FACEBOOK

DATING SECRETS

TECHNIQUES FOR MEN AND WOMEN

RELATIONSHIP INITIATIVE

First Edition 2024

Published by Relationship Initiative

CONTENTS

INTRODUCTION

In this digital age where technology intertwines with every aspect of our lives, it is no surprise that it has also permeated the realm of romance and relationships. Online dating platforms have become the new norm, forever changing the way we meet, connect, and fall in love. Among these platforms, Facebook Dating has emerged as a major player, offering a unique blend of social networking and romantic matchmaking. Welcome to "Facebook Dating Secrets: Techniques For Men and Women".

This book is designed to guide you through the intricate maze of Facebook Dating, providing you with the tools and techniques to successfully navigate this online dating platform. Whether you're a novice entering the online dating world for the first time or a seasoned pro looking for a fresh approach, this book will offer you a treasure trove of insights that will enhance your Facebook Dating experience.

We're here to debunk the mysteries surrounding Facebook Dating, turning it into an exciting journey rather than an intimidating challenge. We understand that online dating can often feel like a gamble, with uncertainty and confusion at every turn. Our goal is to empower both men and women with the knowledge and confidence to not only understand the platform but also to use it in a way that aligns with their unique dating goals and preferences.

From creating an appealing profile, understanding the algorithm, initiating a conversation, to transitioning from online to offline dating, this book covers it all. We'll explore the nuances of online communication, the art of virtual flirting, and the secrets to maintaining interest and building a connection.

So, whether you're seeking a serious relationship, a casual fling, or simply looking to broaden your social circle, let this book be your guide to mastering Facebook Dating. After all, love in the time of technology doesn't have to be complicated. Let's embark on this journey together, unlocking the secrets of Facebook Dating and discovering the endless possibilities it holds.

Chapter 1: Introduction to Facebook Dating

Understanding Online Dating

The advent of the internet has revolutionized the way we connect and interact with others, and dating is no exception. Online dating, once perceived as a last resort for the desperate or socially awkward, has become a ubiquitous part of the modern social landscape. With over 40 million Americans using online dating services, it is clear that this is not just a passing trend but a significant cultural shift.

Enter Facebook Dating, the social media giant's foray into the world of online romance. It is a free feature within the Facebook app, aiming to facilitate meaningful connections and relationships. However, to fully harness the potential of this new platform, we must first understand the broader context of online dating.

Online dating has democratized the pursuit of love and companionship. It provides a platform for individuals of all ages, orientations, and backgrounds to connect based on shared interests and values. It allows you to cast a wider net than traditional dating methods, reaching beyond your immediate social circle or geographic location. With online dating, your next romantic connection could be just a swipe or click away.

Yet, online dating is not without its challenges. It requires a careful balance between presenting an authentic version of yourself and ensuring your safety and privacy. There's also the paradox of choice: the seemingly endless array of potential matches can lead to decision paralysis and constant second-guessing.

This is where Facebook Dating comes in. It leverages the power of social media to create a more authentic and integrated dating experience. Facebook Dating uses the information you've already shared on your profile to help you find potential matches. It also lets you share your live location with a trusted friend when you go on a date, adding an extra layer of safety.

However, as with any online platform, it's essential to approach Facebook Dating with a critical eye. It's important to remember that not everyone may be as they seem online. Moreover, while the platform may use your data to suggest potential matches, it's up to you to decide who you want to connect with.

To make the most of Facebook Dating, you need to understand how to navigate its features effectively. This involves knowing how to set up your dating profile, understanding how the matching algorithm works, and learning how to communicate effectively with potential matches.

The key to successful online dating lies in authenticity, patience, and a willingness to step out of your comfort zone. It's about building genuine connections rather than chasing an idealized notion of romance. And with the right approach and mindset, Facebook Dating could be the tool that helps you find your perfect match.

In conclusion, understanding online dating is the first step towards successfully using Facebook Dating. It's about acknowledging the potential and the pitfalls of this digital landscape. Armed with this knowledge, you can approach Facebook Dating with confidence, ready to connect with others in a meaningful and authentic way. So, are you ready to dive into the exciting world of Facebook Dating? Your next romantic adventure awaits.

Why Choose Facebook Dating

In the vast expanse of online dating platforms, you might wonder, why should you pick Facebook Dating? The answer lies in its blend of simplicity, familiarity, and advanced features, all of which contribute to an enhanced dating experience that is tailored to your preferences and lifestyle.

Firstly, Facebook Dating is built into an application that most of us already use daily - Facebook. There is no need to download a separate app, remember another set of login credentials, or adjust to a new interface. This integration brings a level of convenience that is unparalleled in the realm of online dating. It also saves you precious storage space on your device, which is always a bonus.

Secondly, Facebook Dating leverages the power of the social media giant's vast user base. This means that you have access to a vast pool of potential matches, increasing the likelihood of finding someone who truly resonates with you. Moreover, Facebook's comprehensive user data enables the dating feature to offer highly accurate match suggestions. Instead of spending hours swiping through profiles, you can rely on Facebook's algorithms to connect you with people who share your interests, activities, and even friends.

In addition to this, Facebook Dating prioritizes your safety and privacy. The service is opt-in, meaning your dating profile is separate from your main Facebook profile, and your activity won't be shared with your Facebook friends. It also offers unique features like the ability to share details of your upcoming date with a trusted friend, providing an extra layer of security.

Facebook Dating also offers a refreshing departure from the superficial swiping culture prevalent in many dating apps. Instead of making snap judgments based on profile pictures, Facebook Dating encourages users to delve deeper and get to know potential matches through their profiles. This fosters more meaningful connections and conversations, paving the way for relationships built on shared values and interests, rather than just physical attraction.

What sets Facebook Dating apart is its feature of Secret Crush. This unique feature allows you to select up to nine of your Facebook friends or Instagram followers who you are interested in. If they also happen to use Facebook

Dating and add you to their Secret Crush list, a match is made. This feature adds a fun, exciting element to the online dating experience and offers a way to explore potential relationships within your existing social circles.

Finally, Facebook Dating is a free feature. Unlike many dating apps that require a premium subscription to access certain features, Facebook Dating gives you full access to all its features at no cost. This makes it a cost-effective choice for those who are new to online dating or are wary of investing money in such platforms.

In conclusion, Facebook Dating is a convenient, safe, and effective platform for finding meaningful connections. Its integration with the Facebook app, extensive user base, focus on deep conversations, unique features like Secret Crush, and free access make it a compelling choice in the world of online dating. So, why not give it a shot? You might just find the relationship you've been looking for.

Pros and Cons

While Facebook Dating offers a plethora of opportunities to connect with potential partners, it's important to weigh the benefits against the potential drawbacks. This chapter will explore both the advantages and disadvantages of using this platform as your primary tool for online dating.

On the positive side, Facebook Dating provides a vast pool of potential matches. With more than 2.8 billion active users on Facebook, the dating platform has access to an incredibly diverse and extensive user base. This means that no matter what your preferences are, you're likely to find someone who fits the bill. The algorithm used by Facebook Dating also analyzes your interests, activities, and other data to suggest matches that you might be compatible with, making the process more efficient.

Another advantage is the integration with Facebook's other features. The feature called "Secret Crush" allows you to select up to nine of your Facebook friends or Instagram followers whom you're interested in. If they also add you to their Secret Crush list, Facebook Dating will let both of you know, creating a potential match. This feature offers a unique and less direct way to express interest in someone you already know.

Furthermore, Facebook Dating is a free service. Unlike many other dating platforms that require a premium subscription to access certain features, Facebook Dating does not have any hidden costs. This makes it an attractive option for those who are hesitant to invest money in online dating.

Now, let's consider the potential drawbacks. One of the most significant concerns is privacy. Although Facebook has stated that it keeps your dating profile separate from your main profile, some users may still feel uncomfortable with the idea of sharing their dating activities on a platform that they also use for other aspects of their lives.

There's also the issue of data security. Facebook has had several high-profile data breaches in the past, which raises concerns about how safe your information is on the platform. While Facebook assures that it takes measures to protect user data, it's always wise to be cautious about what information you share.

Another disadvantage is the potential for increased digital distraction. With notifications from Facebook Dating added to those from your regular Facebook account, you might find yourself spending more time on the platform than you'd like. This can be a hindrance to productivity and focus, especially if you're already struggling with screen time management.

Moreover, while Facebook Dating's vast user base is a plus, it could also be a downside. The sheer volume of potential matches can be overwhelming and make the process of finding a suitable partner feel daunting. It can also lead to a paradox of choice, where having too many options makes it harder to make a decision.

In conclusion, Facebook Dating is an intriguing platform that offers numerous advantages, including a large user base, integration with Facebook's features, and no additional costs. However, it also comes with potential drawbacks, such as privacy concerns, data security issues, and the risk of digital distraction. As with any online dating platform, it's important to approach Facebook Dating with a clear understanding of what you're getting into. It's all about balancing the pros and cons to make an informed decision that suits your dating preferences and lifestyle.

How Facebook Dating Works

In the realm of digital dating, Facebook has emerged as a formidable player. While the concept of finding love on Facebook might initially seem perplexing, it's actually a seamless and intuitive process that integrates the best aspects of social media and online dating. Whether you're a seasoned online dater or just dipping your toes into the pool, Facebook Dating offers unique features that can help you find your perfect match.

To begin, Facebook Dating is not a separate app; it's a feature embedded within the Facebook app. This means that you won't need to download anything new, and you'll have the comfort of staying within the familiar Facebook interface. Users can opt into this feature and create a separate dating profile without their Facebook friends knowing. This ensures privacy and avoids any potential awkwardness.

Once you've created your dating profile, Facebook uses its algorithm magic to suggest potential matches. These suggestions are based on your preferences, interests, and other things you do on Facebook. This is where Facebook Dating stands out from other dating apps. It leverages the wealth of information you've already provided on your Facebook profile to help connect you with like-minded individuals.

Moreover, you can also choose to see friends of friends or go outside your friend network for potential matches. This strikes a balance between meeting completely random strangers and dating within your social circle. It's a fresh approach that combines the serendipity of real-life encounters with the convenience of digital dating.

Facebook Dating also introduces an innovative feature called Secret Crush. This allows you to select up to nine of your Facebook friends or Instagram followers who you're interested in. If they've opted into Facebook Dating, they'll get a notification that someone has a crush on them. If they add you to their Secret Crush list too, it's a match! This feature provides a safe and subtle way to express interest in someone you already know.

Safety and control are paramount in Facebook Dating. You can report and block anyone, and Facebook won't suggest your friends or people you've blocked as potential matches. You can also choose whether or not you want to match with friends of your friends. This gives you the power to define your dating experience.

Furthermore, Facebook Dating is free and doesn't include any premium plans or paywalls. This means everyone has equal access to all features, making it a democratic platform for finding love.

In conclusion, Facebook Dating is a sophisticated and user-friendly dating platform. It leverages the power of social networking to help you find love, offering a unique blend of features that prioritize your preferences, safety, and privacy. Whether you're seeking a serious relationship or just testing the waters, Facebook Dating offers an innovative and exciting way to connect with potential partners. Let the world's most popular social media platform play cupid and guide you towards your perfect match.

Getting Started

So, you've decided to plunge into the world of Facebook Dating. Congratulations! This is a big step towards finding the love of your life or simply expanding your social circle. Let's guide you through the initial stages of setting up your profile and navigating this new world.

Firstly, let's debunk a common myth. Many people believe that Facebook Dating is just another version of Facebook. This is not true. Facebook Dating is a separate entity that exists within the main Facebook app. You don't need to create a new Facebook account to use Facebook Dating.

This means your dating activity won't be visible to your Facebook friends unless you choose to share it.

To get started with Facebook Dating, you need to opt-in. This is a simple process. Simply navigate to the Facebook Dating section within your Facebook app and follow the prompts. You'll be asked to set up a Dating Profile, which is separate from your main Facebook profile. Remember, this is your chance to make a great first impression, so choose your photos and write your bio carefully.

When setting up your profile, authenticity is key. Be honest about your interests and what you're looking for. If you love hiking and outdoor adventures, say so. If you're a homebody who loves a good book, don't shy away from sharing this. The magic of Facebook Dating lies in its ability to connect you with people who share your interests.

One of the unique features of Facebook Dating is the Secret Crush option. This allows you to select up to nine of your Facebook friends or Instagram followers who you're interested in. If they also add you to their Secret Crush list, it's a match! This feature takes the guesswork out of expressing interest and can be a fun way to explore potential connections within your existing social circles.

Facebook Dating also offers the ability to add both public and private photos. Public photos are visible to everyone you match with, while private photos can be shared with specific people. This allows you to control who sees what, adding an extra layer of privacy to your dating experience.

Navigating Facebook Dating is a breeze. You're presented with potential matches one at a time and can choose to either pass or express interest. If both parties express interest, it's a match and you can start chatting.

Remember, Facebook Dating is designed to help you find meaningful relationships, not just casual hookups. It's about getting to know people on a deeper level, so take your time. Don't rush the process and don't feel pressured to meet up with someone until you're ready.

In conclusion, getting started with Facebook Dating is a straightforward process. It's about authenticity, taking control of your dating experience, and ultimately, finding meaningful connections. So, why not give it a try? You never know, your perfect match might be just a click away.

Remember, love is a journey, not a destination. Enjoy the ride and have fun exploring the world of Facebook Dating. After all, the best relationships often start with a simple

'Hello'. So go ahead, say 'Hello' and start your journey today.

Chapter 2: Creating a Captivating Profile

Profile Photo Tips

In the world of Facebook dating, a picture indeed speaks a thousand words. Your profile photo is arguably the most critical element of your online dating profile. It's the first thing potential matches will see, and it will significantly influence their decision to engage with you or not. Therefore, it's essential to carefully select your profile photo, ensuring it's not just visually appealing but also communicates the right message about you.

Firstly, your profile photo should be both clear and recent. Blurry or outdated images can be misleading and may create a false impression about you. Remember, honesty is the cornerstone of any successful relationship, and that includes online dating as well. By using a recent and clear photo, you're showing potential matches that you're genuine and open, which can significantly increase your chances of attracting the right people.

Secondly, your profile photo should reflect your personality. If you're a fun-loving, adventurous person, choose a picture that showcases this. Perhaps a photo of you hiking, traveling, or at a music festival. If you're more of a homebody, a picture of you reading a book or cooking might be more appropriate. The goal is to give potential matches an insight into who you are and what you enjoy doing.

Thirdly, be mindful of the background of your photo. A cluttered or messy background can be distracting and take away from the focus of the image, which is you. Opt for a clean, neutral background that enhances your appearance rather than detracting from it.

Next, consider the lighting in your photo. Good lighting can make a world of difference in how you look in an image. Natural light is typically the most flattering, so try to take your profile photo during the day when there's plenty of light. Avoid using harsh, direct light, as this can create unflattering shadows.

Another tip is to avoid using overly edited or filtered photos. While it can be tempting to use filters to enhance your appearance, they can often make your picture look unnatural and can even be off-putting to some people. Instead, opt for a photo that shows the real you.

Moreover, your photo should ideally be a headshot or a waist-up shot. This allows potential matches to clearly see your face, which can help to create a more personal connection. Full-body shots can also be used, but they should be secondary to your main profile picture.

Lastly, when choosing your profile photo, always remember to smile. A warm, genuine smile can make you appear more approachable and friendly, which can significantly boost your chances of attracting potential matches.

In conclusion, your profile photo is your first impression on Facebook dating. It's a visual representation of who you are, and it can either draw people in or push them away. By following these tips, you can ensure that your profile photo is not just attractive but also accurately represents you. Remember, the goal is not just to attract any match, but the right match. So, let your profile photo speak volumes about you and watch as you attract the right people into your online dating life.

Writing an Engaging Bio

To succeed in the realm of Facebook Dating, your bio must be a captivating portrayal of your personality. It's your first and best opportunity to leave a lasting impression. It's your virtual handshake, your introduction, your chance to make a connection. And most importantly, it's the key to unlocking the mysteries of attracting potential partners.

Remember, your bio is not just a summary of your life, it's an advertisement. It's your personal brand. It's your chance to sell yourself, to make yourself irresistible, to make potential partners want to know more about you. This is a golden opportunity to capture their attention, to make them pause and say, "This person seems interesting. I want to know more."

The first step in crafting an engaging bio is to be genuine. Authenticity is attractive. Be true to yourself and your personality. There's no point in pretending to be someone you're not, as the truth will eventually come out. Be proud of who you are and let your true self shine through.

Next, use humor. Humor is a universal language that can bridge gaps and break down barriers. It's a surefire way to catch someone's attention and make your bio memorable. Everyone loves someone who can make them laugh. But remember, the key is to be subtle. You're not trying to be a stand-up comedian, just someone who doesn't take life too seriously.

Keep it short and sweet. Your bio should be concise but impactful. Don't ramble on about your life story. Instead, focus on a few key aspects of your life that you think are worth sharing. This could be your hobbies, your job, or something unique about you. Remember, the goal is to pique their interest, not to give everything away.

Use your bio to showcase your interests and passions. This not only gives potential partners a glimpse into your world, but also provides conversation starters. Sharing your love for travel, your culinary skills, or your passion for photography can spark interest and initiate meaningful conversations.

Avoid clichés and be original. Phrases like "I love to laugh" or "I enjoy long walks on the beach" are overused and unimpressive. Instead, try to paint a vivid picture of who you are and what you love in an original and unique way.

Lastly, be positive. Nobody wants to date a pessimist. Positivity is attractive and infectious. Your bio should reflect a positive outlook on life. Avoid mentioning past relationships or anything that might come across as negative.

Remember, your bio is the first impression you make on potential partners. It's your chance to stand out from the crowd, to be memorable, to be desirable. It's your opportunity to showcase your personality, your interests, and your passions. It's your chance to make a connection, to spark interest, to make them want to know more.

So take your time, put some thought into it, and craft a bio that truly represents you. It might just be the key to unlocking the secrets of Facebook Dating. Remember, you're not just writing a bio, you're creating a brand, a brand that's all about you. So make it count.

Hobbies and Interests

As you navigate the intriguing world of Facebook Dating, it's crucial to understand the role your hobbies and interests play in attracting potential matches. These seemingly trivial details paint a vibrant picture of who you are and what you enjoy, serving as an ice-breaker, a conversation starter, and a compatibility indicator.

Think about it. Would you rather engage with an individual whose profile is as bland as an unseasoned dish or someone whose interests resonate with yours, sparking intrigue and curiosity? The answer is obvious. Your interests can act as a magnet, attracting like-minded individuals and paving the way for meaningful connections.

Now, you might wonder, "What if my hobbies are too specific or uncommon?" Fear not. In the vast universe of Facebook Dating, there are individuals who share your passion for collecting rare stamps, your love for underwater basket weaving, or your fascination with quantum physics. By sharing your unique interests, you stand out from the crowd, making it easier for your soulmate to find you amidst the sea of generic profiles.

Furthermore, expressing your hobbies and interests allows you to showcase your individuality. In a platform where thousands of profiles compete for attention, your distinct hobbies can be your unique selling point. It's like a beacon of authenticity in a realm often marred by pretentiousness. It signals that you are not just another face in the crowd, but an individual with depth and character.

Moreover, sharing your interests serves as a litmus test for compatibility. It's not just about attracting anyone; it's about attracting the right one. Your shared love for indie films, vegan cuisine, or hiking adventures could be the common ground that strengthens your connection. It could be the foundation of countless dates, shared experiences, and intimate moments.

However, it's critical to present your hobbies in a compelling manner. Instead of merely listing your interests, narrate a story. If you love painting, discuss the first time you held a brush, the thrill of mixing colors, the tranquility it brings. If you're into rock climbing, share the adrenaline rush, the stunning views at the peak, the life lessons it taught you. By doing so, you're not just sharing a hobby; you're sharing a piece of your world.

In addition, balance is key. While it's important to share your passions, avoid coming across as a one-trick pony. Show that you're a well-rounded individual with diverse interests. This suggests that you're adaptable, open to new experiences, and capable of maintaining stimulating conversations on various topics.

To sum it up, your hobbies and interests are a powerful tool in Facebook Dating. They create a vivid image of your personality, highlight your uniqueness, and serve as a filter for compatibility. They add color to your profile, making it more engaging and relatable. So, don't underestimate these details. Use them to your advantage, and watch as they transform your dating game, leading you closer to your ideal match.

Displaying Your Lifestyle

Living a life that is true to yourself not only brings happiness but also attracts people who appreciate you for who you are. On Facebook Dating, showcasing your lifestyle is an integral part of making a genuine connection. This chapter will guide you on how to effectively portray your lifestyle and attract the right partner.

Firstly, it's essential to understand that your lifestyle consists of your interests, hobbies, values, and habits. It is what makes you unique, setting you apart from the rest. When you display your lifestyle on Facebook Dating, you're giving potential partners a glimpse into your world, allowing them to decide if they'd like to be a part of it.

Start by updating your profile pictures and cover photos with images that represent your lifestyle. If you're an adventurer who loves hiking, upload pictures of yourself in the mountains. If you're a foodie, show pictures of your culinary adventures. If you're an artist, showcase your artwork. Let your pictures tell your story.

Next, your posts and status updates are another great way to display your lifestyle. Share posts about the books you're reading, the music you're listening to, or the places you've traveled to. Your posts should reflect your interests and values. Remember, your goal is to attract someone who shares or respects your lifestyle.

In addition, participate in Facebook groups that align with your lifestyle. If you're a fitness enthusiast, join fitness groups. If you're passionate about environmental conservation, join groups that focus on this topic. Participating in such groups not only displays your lifestyle but also increases your chances of meeting like-minded individuals.

However, it's crucial to be authentic. Presenting an exaggerated or false version of your lifestyle might attract attention in the short term, but it won't lead to meaningful or lasting connections. People appreciate honesty and are more likely to be attracted to someone who is genuine.

Also, while it's important to showcase your lifestyle, remember not to overshare. Maintain some level of privacy. This creates an aura of mystery, making you more intriguing to potential partners. It also ensures that you have more to talk about during your conversations.

Moreover, remember that your lifestyle is not static. As you grow and evolve, so should your portrayal of your lifestyle on Facebook Dating. Regularly update your profile and posts to reflect changes in your lifestyle. This shows that you're a dynamic individual who embraces growth and change.

Finally, be proud of your lifestyle. Whether you're a night owl or an early bird, a homebody or a social butterfly, there's someone out there who will appreciate you for who you are. By displaying your lifestyle authentically, you're not only attracting potential partners but also asserting your identity and reinforcing your self-esteem.

In conclusion, displaying your lifestyle on Facebook Dating is not just about finding a partner. It's also about expressing your identity, connecting with like-minded individuals, and celebrating the life you lead. So, go ahead and showcase your lifestyle. Who knows, your perfect match might just be a click away.

Privacy and Safety

In the exciting world of Facebook Dating, it is crucial to prioritize privacy and safety above all. After all, protecting your personal and sensitive information should always come first, even when you are looking for your soulmate. As we delve deeper into the secrets of Facebook Dating, we must stress the importance of safeguarding your privacy and safety.

Many people feel apprehensive about online dating due to concerns about privacy and safety. However, Facebook Dating has implemented several features that ensure you can search for love without compromising your security. It's time to erase those worries and embrace the opportunities that Facebook Dating brings to the table.

Facebook Dating is designed to protect your privacy. Unlike other dating platforms, it does not create a public dating profile that everyone can see. Only those who have opted into the Facebook Dating service can view your dating profile. This means your friends, family, and coworkers on Facebook won't stumble across your dating activities. You are in control of who sees your dating profile, which gives you a higher level of privacy.

Furthermore, Facebook Dating doesn't allow users to send pictures or links to prevent unsolicited and inappropriate content from being shared. This is a significant step towards ensuring a safer dating environment. In addition, the ability to report and block anyone who makes you uncomfortable provides an extra layer of protection.

One of the most unique safety features of Facebook Dating is the ability to share details of your upcoming date with a trusted friend or family member using the "Share Your Plans" feature. This includes the time, location, and the name of the person you are meeting. In case of any unforeseen circumstances, someone will have information about your whereabouts. This feature provides a sense of security when meeting someone new for the first time.

It is also important to remember that your safety and privacy are not entirely in the hands of Facebook Dating. You also have a role to play. Be cautious about the information you share on your profile and in your conversations. Avoid sharing sensitive information such as your home address, workplace, phone number, or financial details. It's always better to be safe than sorry.

Moreover, always listen to your gut feeling. If someone seems suspicious or if something doesn't feel right, it probably isn't. Don't hesitate to report or block someone if you feel threatened or uncomfortable. Your safety should always be your top priority.

Remember, finding love should never compromise your safety and privacy. With Facebook Dating, you can enjoy the journey of finding your perfect match while feeling secure and protected. So go ahead, dip your toes into the world of Facebook Dating, and you might just find the love you've been waiting for all along.

In conclusion, Facebook Dating is not just about bringing people together; it's about doing so in a safe and private environment. So take the plunge, enjoy the experience, but always keep your safety and privacy at the forefront. After all, the best love story is one where you feel safe, secure, and respected.

Chapter 3: Understanding Facebook's Dating Algorithm

How the Algorithm Works

Before diving into the secrets of Facebook Dating, it is crucial to understand its backbone – the algorithm. The algorithm, in simple terms, is a set of rules or processes that the platform uses to sort, categorize, and present data to its users. It's not just a cold, mathematical formula but a dynamic and ever-evolving mechanism designed to create a more personalized and rewarding experience for you.

The Facebook Dating algorithm, specifically, is the cupid's bow that seeks to match you with potential partners based on your preferences, activities, and interactions. It's not as simple as matching two people who like the same music or have the same hobbies. It's a complex system that takes into account a multitude of factors to ensure a high degree of compatibility.

Facebook Dating doesn't just rely on your 'likes' or 'shares'. It delves deeper, analyzing your interests, your interactions with others, your listed preferences, and even the level of activity on your profile. It's an intricate web of data that collectively builds a comprehensive picture of who you are and who might be your ideal match.

The algorithm's magic lies in its ability to learn and adapt. The more you use Facebook Dating, the more it 'understands' you. It observes your behavior - who you interact with, what kind of profiles you tend to like, your response to suggested matches, and so on. With each interaction, it becomes more refined, enhancing its ability to suggest potential partners that align with your preferences and personality.

But it's not all about you. The algorithm also considers the other person's preferences and activities. It's a two-way street, ensuring both parties have a mutual interest and compatibility. It's not just about finding someone you like; it's about finding someone who also likes you back.

Moreover, it's important to remember that the algorithm is designed to encourage meaningful connections. It doesn't prioritize physical appearance or superficial attributes. Instead, it focuses on shared interests, mutual friends, and common activities – factors that contribute to a deeper, more meaningful connection.

The Facebook Dating algorithm is a powerful tool, but it's not infallible. It's not a magic wand that will find your perfect match with a single swipe. It's a tool that aids in your journey, but the ultimate decision still lies with you. It's essential to approach it with an open mind and a willingness to explore.

In essence, the Facebook Dating algorithm is your silent, digital wingman. It's there to guide you, to help you navigate the complex world of online dating. But remember, it's not the algorithm that makes the connection; it's you. It's your conversations, your shared laughs, your mutual interests that will ultimately ignite the spark.

Understanding how the algorithm works is the first step in harnessing its power. It's the key to unlocking the secrets of Facebook Dating, to navigating its virtual corridors in search of your perfect match. With this knowledge, you can make informed decisions, optimize your profile, and enhance your chances of finding that special someone.

So, ready to dive in? Let's unravel the secrets of Facebook Dating together.

Maximizing Your Visibility

Expanding your reach on Facebook Dating is not only about crafting an attractive profile, but it's also about increasing your visibility. Your chances of finding the perfect match multiply when you are more visible to potential partners. However, the question that arises is, how can you maximize your visibility?

Firstly, be active. A dormant profile is as good as no profile. Regular activity on your account is a surefire way to increase your visibility. Engage in the platform, respond to messages promptly, and don't let conversations die down. Facebook's algorithm recognizes active users and rewards them with increased visibility.

Secondly, utilize the power of profile pictures. A picture is truly worth a thousand words, and in the world of online dating, it might be worth a thousand dates. Your profile picture should not only be attractive but also reflective of who you are. It's the first impression you make, so make it count.

Additionally, make use of Facebook's features to maximize your visibility. The 'Secret Crush' option allows you to select up to nine Facebook friends or Instagram followers you're interested in. If your crush adds you to their Secret

Crush list too, it's a match! This feature not only boosts your visibility but also provides a potential love connection.

The 'Stories' feature is another excellent tool for increasing your visibility. Sharing your day-to-day life, interests, and passions can make you more relatable and attractive to potential matches. It's a way to show your personality and make you stand out from the crowd.

Furthermore, be open about your preferences. Facebook Dating allows you to customize your dating preferences. The more specific you are about your interests and what you're looking for, the more likely you are to attract like-minded individuals.

Another effective way to maximize your visibility is by joining Facebook Groups and attending Facebook Events. These platforms provide an opportunity to meet people with similar interests. It's also a way to show that you're sociable and active, qualities that are attractive to potential matches.

Lastly, being genuine and authentic is critical. Authenticity resonates with people and makes you more attractive. Avoid misleading information or fake pictures as they can harm your reputation and decrease your visibility in the long run.

Remember, maximizing your visibility on Facebook Dating is not about being the loudest or the most popular. It's about strategically using the platform's features to your advantage and presenting yourself in a way that is true to who you are.

So, take the plunge, be active, utilize Facebook's features, be open about your preferences, join groups and events, and most importantly, be yourself. Your perfect match might just be a few clicks away.

In conclusion, maximizing your visibility on Facebook Dating is about being proactive and utilizing the platform's features to your advantage. It's about presenting a genuine image of yourself and engaging with potential matches. So don't wait, take the reins of your love life and maximize your visibility on Facebook Dating. Your perfect match might just be around the corner!

Managing Your Preferences

If you're serious about finding love on Facebook Dating, the key lies in effectively managing your preferences. The beauty of this platform is that it allows you to tailor your dating experience to meet your unique needs and desires. It's like having a personal matchmaker at your fingertips, capable of filtering through the masses and delivering only the most suitable matches to your screen.

When it comes to setting your preferences, it's crucial to be genuine and honest. Remember, the goal here is not to attract as many matches as possible, but to attract the right ones. Be clear about your intentions and what you're looking for in a partner. If you're seeking a serious relationship, make sure to indicate that. If you're more interested in casual dating or friendships, that's perfectly fine too. The important thing is to be true to yourself and your desires.

Your preferences should also reflect your non-negotiables. These are the things you absolutely cannot compromise on in a relationship. Maybe it's a certain level of education, a particular faith, or a specific lifestyle. Whatever it is, don't be afraid to set these as your standards. You're not being too picky; you're simply being smart about your dating choices.

But while it's important to be firm on your non-negotiables, it's equally important to be flexible on other aspects. You might prefer tall, dark, and handsome, but don't let that stop you from considering someone who might be short, fair, and charming. In other words, don't get too hung up on superficial preferences. Focus on what really matters: shared values, compatible personalities, and mutual respect and understanding.

Another significant aspect of managing your preferences is updating them regularly. As you interact with different people and go on dates, you'll gain a better understanding of what you truly want in a partner. Maybe you'll realize that a good sense of humor is more important to you than physical attractiveness. Or perhaps you'll discover that you value ambition more than you thought. Use these insights to refine your preferences and improve your chances of finding the perfect match.

Moreover, don't forget to pay attention to the preferences of your potential matches as well. Respect their choices and understand that they're looking for certain qualities just like you are. If you don't meet their criteria, don't take it personally. Instead, see it as an opportunity to find someone who truly appreciates you for who you are.

Finally, remember that managing your preferences is not a one-time activity. It's an ongoing process that requires regular reflection and adjustment. As you grow and evolve, so will your preferences. Embrace this change and let it guide you in your journey to find love.

In conclusion, managing your preferences effectively is a crucial part of your Facebook Dating experience. It's an opportunity to be honest about your desires, to set your standards, and to remain open to unexpected possibilities. It's also a chance to learn more about yourself and what you truly value in a relationship. So, take charge of your preferences and let them lead you to your perfect match. After all, the power to find love is in your hands.

Dealing with Limited Matches

Imagine this: you've set up your Facebook Dating profile to perfection. Your photos are stunning, your bio is witty and engaging, and you're ready to dive into the world of online dating. Yet, as you eagerly wait for potential matches, you notice something disheartening: the number of matches you're getting is less than expected. This situation might feel like a blow to your confidence, but don't let it discourage you. It's not about the quantity, but the quality of matches that truly matters.

In the grand scheme of dating, it's not about how many fish you can reel in but about catching the right one. Having a limited number of matches can be a blessing in disguise, allowing you to devote your attention to a select few and ensuring you don't spread yourself too thin. It provides the opportunity to invest time in getting to know your matches on a deeper level, fostering a connection that is built on more than just appearances.

The first step in dealing with limited matches is to adjust your mindset. You must understand that this is not a reflection of your worth or attractiveness. The algorithms of dating apps are complex, and the number of matches you receive can depend on various factors, many of which are beyond your control. It's more productive to focus on the matches you do have rather than worrying about the ones you don't.

Next, take advantage of the limited matches by using them as an opportunity to refine your approach to online dating. Each interaction is a chance to learn and grow, to better understand what you're looking for in a partner and how to communicate effectively. Use each match as a stepping stone towards becoming more confident and adept at navigating the online dating world.

Moreover, having limited matches encourages you to be more selective. It forces you to truly consider each potential partner, to weigh their attributes and compatibility with you, rather than mindlessly swiping right. This selective approach can lead to more meaningful relationships, as you're more likely to match with those you genuinely connect with.

However, if you find that the quantity of matches is consistently low, it might be worth revisiting your profile. Perhaps your photos could be updated, or your bio could be more engaging. Remember, your profile is your first impression, so make it count.

Finally, don't let the fear of limited matches discourage you from exploring Facebook Dating. The platform offers numerous features designed to help you find your perfect match, such as the ability to match with people who share similar interests or are attending the same events. These unique aspects can make your dating experience more enjoyable and successful.

In conclusion, dealing with limited matches on Facebook Dating is not a setback but an opportunity. It's a chance to refocus your approach, to be more selective, and to build stronger connections with your matches. Remember, it's not a numbers game; it's about finding the right person for you. So, stay positive, keep refining your profile, and most importantly, enjoy the journey of online dating.

Algorithm Myths Debunked

Many people are under the misguided belief that there is a mysterious, complex algorithm governing Facebook Dating. They're convinced that this algorithm is an all-powerful entity, intricately controlling their chances of finding love online. This kind of thinking, while understandable, is largely a myth. Let's debunk some of these myths and shed some light on the realities of Facebook Dating.

Firstly, the notion that Facebook Dating uses a complex algorithm to match users is, to some degree, true. However, it's not as mystical or complicated as you might think. The algorithm primarily uses your preferences, interests, and interactions on Facebook to suggest potential matches. It does not, contrary to popular belief, have an agenda or premeditated design to keep you single or ruin your love life.

Another common misconception is that the more active you are, the better your chances of being matched. While your activity does contribute to the algorithm's understanding of your interests, it doesn't necessarily mean you'll get more or better matches. Quality over quantity is the key here. Engage meaningfully with your interests on Facebook, and the algorithm is likely to suggest matches who share these interests.

The idea that you can 'game' the algorithm by liking certain pages, interacting with certain posts, or changing your activity is another myth that needs debunking. The algorithm is designed to adapt and learn from your behavior over time. Any short-term changes you make are unlikely to have a significant impact on your suggested matches. It's more beneficial to be authentic and let the algorithm learn from your genuine interests and activities.

The belief that the algorithm favors attractive people is another widely held, but incorrect assumption. Facebook Dating does not rank users based on physical appearance. It's designed to facilitate meaningful connections based on shared interests and mutual preferences, not superficial attractiveness.

One final myth to debunk is the idea that the algorithm is somehow 'against' you. This is simply not the case. The algorithm is a tool, not an adversary. It's designed to help you find potential matches based on your activity and preferences. If you're not finding the right matches, it might be worth revisiting your preferences or the way you engage with Facebook.

In conclusion, while Facebook Dating does use an algorithm to suggest potential matches, many of the myths surrounding it are based on misconceptions and misinformation. The algorithm is not a mystical entity with an agenda, but a tool designed to help you find potential matches based on your genuine interests and activities. So, engage authentically, be true to your interests, and let the algorithm do its job. After all, love isn't a game to be won by tricking the system, but a journey to be embarked upon with honesty and openness.

Chapter 4: Starting Engaging Conversations

First Message Do's and Don'ts

Imagine you're standing in front of a vast ocean of potential partners, each one more intriguing than the last. The realm of Facebook Dating is like this limitless sea, teeming with individuals who could be your perfect match. But how do you make that first move? What do you say to capture their interest and stand out from the crowd? The first message is your chance to make a lasting impression, and it's crucial to get it right.

In the world of online dating, the first message is equivalent to your first physical meeting. It's your initial handshake, your opening smile; it's your chance to show your personality and spark interest. So, let's dive into the do's and don'ts of that all-important first message.

Do be original and personal. Remember, the person on the other side of that screen is just like you, a human being looking for connection. They want to feel seen and valued, not like they're one of a hundred copy-pasted messages.

Take the time to read their profile, find shared interests, or comment on something unique about them. This shows you're genuinely interested and not just playing a numbers game.

Don't be overly familiar or invasive. While it's great to show interest, there's a line between being interested and being intrusive. Avoid commenting on physical appearance or asking too personal questions in your first interaction. This can come off as creepy or desperate and is likely to make the other person uncomfortable.

Do use humor. A well-placed joke or witty remark can be a great ice breaker. It shows you don't take yourself too seriously and can make the other person smile. Just make sure your humor is light-hearted and not offensive or overly sarcastic.

Don't use cliche lines or generic compliments. "You have beautiful eyes" or "I never do this, but..." has been heard a thousand times before. It's impersonal and, frankly, unimpressive. Instead, try to comment on something specific about their profile or photos.

Do be respectful and polite. Remember, this is your first impression. You want to come off as a kind and considerate person, not someone who's rude or disrespectful. This includes avoiding offensive language or comments.

Don't send a novel. While it's important to show you've read their profile and have genuine interest, there's no need to write an essay. Keep your message concise and to the point. This makes it more likely they will read it and respond.

Do proofread your message. Spelling and grammar mistakes can be a huge turn-off. They give the impression that you're careless or not really interested. A well-written message shows you've put effort into it and care about making a good impression.

Don't be discouraged if you don't get a response. Not everyone will be a match, and that's okay. Keep trying, keep refining your approach, and remember, every no brings you one step closer to a yes.

The first message in Facebook Dating is a crucial step in your journey to find love online. By following these simple do's and don'ts, you'll increase your chances of making a positive first impression and starting a conversation that could lead to something special. So take a deep breath, be yourself, and dive into the exciting world of Facebook Dating.

Keeping the Conversation Going

You've made the first move, and there's a spark. Now, how do you fan that spark into a flame? It's time to master the art of keeping the conversation going. The key to successful Facebook dating isn't just about making a great first impression; it's about sustaining interest and building a connection.

The cornerstone of a captivating conversation is curiosity. Show genuine interest in your potential partner. Ask open-ended questions that stimulate thought and evoke emotions. For instance, rather than asking, "Do you like music?" (to which the answer may simply be "yes" or "no"), ask, "What kind of music moves you, and why?" This not only keeps the conversation going but also opens up avenues for you to explore shared interests or discover new ones.

Remember, communication is a two-way street. While you want to keep your partner engaged, it's equally important for you to contribute to the conversation. Share stories, experiences, and ideas that can help your potential partner understand you better. However, be mindful not to dominate the conversation. Striking a balance between talking and listening is crucial in maintaining a healthy dialogue.

Now, let's talk about timing. In the fast-paced world of social media, it's tempting to respond immediately. But, it's important to remember that desperation is not attractive. Take your time to craft a thoughtful response. This communicates that you value the conversation and are invested in it.

On the other hand, don't leave your potential partner hanging for too long. Delaying your response excessively can send the wrong message. The goal is to keep the conversation flowing naturally. So, find a rhythm that works for both of you.

In Facebook dating, emojis can be your best friends. They add color and emotion to your messages, making them more personal and expressive. A well-placed smiley can lighten the mood, while a heart emoji can subtly express affection. But, like everything else, moderation is key.

Overdoing it can make your messages seem insincere or juvenile.

Additionally, be mindful of the tone of your messages. Sarcasm and humor can be tricky to convey through text. What you might find funny, your potential partner might find offensive. So, until you've established a comfort level, it's best to keep the conversation light and positive.

Another secret to keeping the conversation going is to leave it on a high note, with something for your potential partner to look forward to. This could be a thought-provoking question, a funny anecdote, or a teaser for your next conversation. This not only keeps your partner intrigued but also gives you a conversation starter for next time.

Lastly, be patient. Building a connection takes time. Don't rush the process. Take the time to get to know each other, enjoy the conversation, and let the relationship bloom naturally.

In Facebook dating, the conversation is the key to unlocking a potential relationship. So, make every word count. Be genuine, be patient, and most importantly, be yourself. After all, the best conversations are the ones that are honest, engaging, and effortless.

Topic Ideas for Conversations

Diving into the world of Facebook Dating can be an exhilarating adventure. Yet, it can also be a daunting task, especially when it comes to initiating engaging conversations. Fear not, for here are some compelling topic ideas that will not only break the ice but also help you connect on a deeper level.

Let's start with the most fundamental yet effective approach – common interests. Facebook Dating allows you to see your potential match's likes and interests. Use this to your advantage. Have they liked a particular band, movie, or book? Do they follow certain sports or have a penchant for cooking? Use these topics as a springboard to initiate a conversation. "I see you're a fan of 'The Office.' Who's your favorite character?" or "You seem to love cooking. What's your signature dish?" Not only does this show that you have taken the time to look at their profile, but it also opens up a world of shared interests and experiences.

Next, let's talk about the power of open-ended questions. Instead of asking yes or no questions, ask something that prompts a more detailed response. For instance, "What's the best book you've read recently and why?" or "What was your most memorable travel experience?" This will give your potential match an opportunity to share more about themselves, and their answers will provide you with more topics to explore.

Remember, everyone loves a good story. So, why not ask about their personal anecdotes? Questions like, "What's the funniest thing that's happened to you recently?" or "Tell me about a moment when you felt really proud of yourself," not only make the conversation more engaging but also allow you to get to know the person behind the profile.

Now, let's not forget about current affairs. Facebook Dating provides a unique feature where you can share content from your Facebook feed with your matches. This can be a great conversation starter. Shared an article about a recent scientific discovery? Ask their thoughts on it. Posted a funny meme? Use it to bring out their sense of humor.

Moreover, while it's important to keep the conversation light and fun, don't shy away from deeper subjects. Ask about their life goals, their values, their dreams. This not only shows that you're interested in knowing them on a deeper level, but it also helps you assess your compatibility.

Lastly, remember that the best conversations are two-way streets. Share your own stories, experiences, and thoughts. Open yourself up and let them see the person behind the profile.

In conclusion, initiating a conversation on Facebook Dating doesn't have to be a daunting task. With these topic ideas, you'll be able to keep the conversation flowing and get to know your potential match on a deeper level. Remember, it's not about impressing them with your wit or knowledge. It's about creating a connection, a bond. So, be genuine, be curious, be yourself. Happy dating!

Dealing with Ghosting

As you navigate the exciting and somewhat nerve-wracking world of Facebook Dating, you may encounter a phenomenon known as 'ghosting.' This is when someone you've been interacting with suddenly disappears without explanation, ceasing all communication. It's a digital vanishing act that leaves you questioning, confused, and potentially hurt. Ghosting is a shared experience in the modern dating world, but it doesn't make it any less distressing. However, it's crucial to understand how to deal with ghosting effectively and healthily.

Firstly, it's essential to remember that ghosting is more reflective of the person who does it than the person who experiences it. It's an act of emotional immaturity and a lack of consideration for others' feelings. If someone ghosts you, it's a clear sign that they were not ready for a mature, respectful relationship. In this context, ghosting can be seen as a blessing in disguise, saving you from investing more time and emotion in someone incapable of meeting your needs.

It's natural to feel upset or even angry when you've been ghosted. However, resist the urge to seek closure by confronting the ghoster. The act of ghosting itself reveals that they probably lack the emotional maturity to provide you with the closure you seek. Instead, focus on self-care and surround yourself with supportive friends and family. Engage in activities that you enjoy and that boost your mood. Remember, your worth is not defined by someone else's inability to see it.

While it's essential to take time to heal, don't let the experience of being ghosted deter you from future dating. Not everyone will treat you this way, and it's crucial not to let one negative experience taint your perspective on dating as a whole. Approach new connections with an open mind and heart, but also learn from your experience. Take things slow, and don't be afraid to communicate your needs and expectations early on.

When using Facebook Dating, be mindful of red flags that could indicate a potential ghoster. These might include inconsistent communication patterns, reluctance to meet in person or video chat, and vague or non-committal responses to your questions about their life or your future together. By staying alert to these signs, you can potentially save yourself from the heartache of being ghosted.

Lastly, remember that it's okay to take a break from dating if you need to. If you've been ghosted and it's affected you deeply, taking some time for yourself can be beneficial. Use this time to reflect on what you want in a partner and a relationship, and return to the dating scene when you feel ready and confident.

Ghosting is a painful reality of modern dating, but it's not a reflection of your worth or desirability. By understanding how to deal with it, you can emerge stronger, wiser, and more prepared for the ups and downs of the dating world. Remember, every experience, good or bad, is a stepping stone towards finding the right person for you. Don't let ghosting deter you from your journey towards love and companionship.

Moving the Conversation Offline

As you navigate the captivating realm of Facebook dating, there comes a point where you must take the conversation off the digital platform and into the real world. This step is crucial. It's the bridge between your online interactions and a potential real-life relationship. However, it's important to tread with caution, wisdom, and a dash of creativity.

Shifting from online to offline might seem daunting. You've grown accustomed to the comfort and convenience of chatting behind a screen. But remember, the goal of Facebook dating isn't to have a long-term relationship on the app; it's to meet someone with whom you can form a genuine connection.

To make this transition smooth, you must first ensure that you and your match are on the same page. It's important to read the cues your match is giving you. If they seem eager to meet in person and the conversation flows naturally, it's probably the right time to propose a meeting. However, if they seem hesitant or reserved, give them some space. It's crucial to respect their comfort zone.

When proposing to move the conversation offline, be direct but considerate. You could say, "I've really enjoyed our conversations and would love to continue them in person. What do you think about meeting up for a coffee?" This approach is straightforward, yet it leaves room for your match to decline politely if they aren't ready.

It's also important to consider safety. Meet in a public place, let someone know where you're going, and don't feel pressured to reveal personal information too quickly. Taking these precautions doesn't mean you're paranoid; it means you're smart.

Once you've set the date, it's time to prepare. Think back to your conversations. What are their interests? What do you have in common? These topics will help keep the conversation flowing when you meet. Remember, the aim isn't to impress them, but to connect with them.

At the meeting, be yourself. Authenticity is key. It's easy to be someone else online, but in real life, pretenses are hard to maintain. Let them see the real you - the one that laughs at corny jokes, the one that loves old-school rock, the one that can't resist a good book.

The transition from online to offline is a significant step, but it doesn't have to be a nerve-wracking one. It's an opportunity to take your connection to the next level. It's a chance to turn your virtual relationship into a tangible one.

Remember, the beauty of Facebook dating lies in its ability to connect you with people who share your interests and values, but the real magic happens when you take the conversation offline. So, when you feel the time is right, take the leap. You never know where it might lead you.

In conclusion, moving the conversation offline is an exciting, essential part of Facebook dating. It's your chance to turn a digital connection into a real-life relationship. So, approach it with confidence, wisdom, and a sprinkle of excitement. After all, this could be the start of something beautiful.

Chapter 5: Maintaining Online Relationships

Keeping the Spark Alive

In the realm of romance, maintaining the spark is as crucial as igniting it in the first place. This is especially true when it comes to Facebook dating, where the digital platform can either fuel the flames of passion or extinguish them with a single click. Keeping your relationship exciting and fresh amidst the monotony of likes, comments, and shares requires a certain level of finesse and understanding of the online dating world.

The first secret to keeping the spark alive is communication. Never underestimate the power of words in a platform where written communication is king. Regular chats, thoughtful messages, and engaging comments on their posts can make your partner feel special and valued. However, remember that quality always trumps quantity. It's not about bombarding them with messages, but about sending meaningful words that can touch their heart and reflect your genuine interest.

Next, harness the power of photos and videos. Facebook dating is a visual experience, and sharing snapshots of your life can create a sense of intimacy. Whether it's a picture of your favorite coffee shop, a video of your pet's latest antics, or a throwback photo from your childhood, these glimpses into your world can help your partner feel closer to you. But be careful not to overshare; maintaining a sense of mystery can lead to more curiosity and engagement.

Another secret is to use Facebook's features to your advantage. Tagging your partner in posts, sharing songs or articles that remind you of them, or using Facebook's dating app features to send them a virtual gift can make them feel special and remembered. These small gestures can make a big difference in keeping the flame of your relationship burning brightly.

However, don't let your online interactions replace real-life experiences. Remember, Facebook is a tool to enhance your relationship, not the sole platform for it. Plan real-life dates, phone calls, and video chats. The thrill of hearing their voice, seeing their smile, or anticipating a date can keep the excitement high in your relationship.

Privacy is another crucial aspect to consider. In the world of Facebook dating, it's easy to cross the line between sharing and oversharing. Be respectful of your partner's privacy and make sure to discuss what is okay to share publicly and what should remain between the two of you. This not only protects your relationship but also builds trust.

Lastly, don't forget to have fun. Facebook dating should not feel like a chore or a job. It should be an exciting, enjoyable part of your life. Share jokes, play online games together, participate in Facebook challenges, or create a joint playlist. These shared experiences can bring joy and spark into your relationship.

Keeping the spark alive in Facebook dating is not rocket science. It's about understanding the digital platform, respecting each other's boundaries, and using the tools at your disposal to maintain a vibrant, exciting relationship. So, go ahead, explore the secrets of Facebook dating, and keep that spark alive!

Managing Expectations

In the quest for genuine connection and lasting love on Facebook Dating, it's crucial to navigate the terrain with a clear and realistic understanding of what to expect. This isn't about stifling your excitement or quelling those butterflies in your stomach. Rather, it's about equipping yourself with the right mindset to handle the highs and lows of online dating.

Firstly, understand that not everyone you meet on Facebook Dating will be your perfect match. There are over 2 billion users on Facebook, and with such a vast pool, you're bound to encounter a diverse range of personalities. It's a journey of sorting, and it's crucial to maintain an open mind while also staying true to your standards and values.

Remember, every conversation or date is not a promise of a lifelong commitment. It's simply an opportunity to get to know someone better. Don't rush into relationships or force connections. Allow them to evolve naturally. Be patient with the process and with yourself.

Secondly, don't let rejection deter you. It's an inevitable part of the dating process, and it's essential to handle it with grace. If someone doesn't respond to your message or declines your invitation for a date, it's not a reflection of your worth. It's merely an indication that you might not be a good match, and that's okay.

It's also important to manage your own actions and reactions. Be mindful not to lead anyone on if you're not interested. Be respectful and clear in your communication. Remember, it's not just about finding the right person, but also about being the right person.

Moreover, be aware that people may present themselves differently online than they are in reality. It's easy to fall for a well-crafted profile or a highlight reel of someone's life. Always take the time to get to know someone beyond their online persona.

Being cautious doesn't mean being cynical. It's about understanding that people are complex, and it takes time and effort to truly know someone. Don't let the flashy profiles and seemingly perfect lives fool you. Real connection lies in shared values, compatibility, and mutual respect.

Lastly, remember that Facebook Dating is merely a tool, a platform. It can't guarantee instant love or a perfect relationship. It's up to you to use this tool effectively. Be genuine in your interactions, be clear about what you're looking for, and most importantly, enjoy the process.

Facebook Dating offers a world of possibilities. It can open doors to potential partners you might not have met otherwise. But it's not a magic solution to finding love. Like any form of dating, it requires effort, patience, and resilience.

As you embark on this journey, remember to manage your expectations. Embrace the process with an open heart and a clear mind. Learn from each interaction, whether it leads to a meaningful connection or a lesson in what you're truly looking for.

So, go ahead, delve into the world of Facebook Dating. But remember, it's not just about the destination, it's about the journey. And who knows, your journey might just lead you to the love you've been searching for.

Dealing with Online Dating Fatigue

Online dating can be an exhilarating adventure, but it's not without its challenges. One of the most common issues people face is online dating fatigue. This phenomenon occurs when you've been on the dating apps for a while, and you're starting to feel worn out. Every profile starts to look the same, and every conversation feels like a chore. If you're feeling this way, don't worry; it's entirely normal and, more importantly, fixable.

Firstly, it's essential to understand that it's okay to take breaks. Online dating is not a job; it's supposed to be fun and exciting. If it's starting to feel like a tiresome task, it's time to step back and take a break. You don't owe anyone an explanation for your absence. Your mental health should always be your priority, and if online dating is causing more stress than joy, it's time to hit the pause button.

During your break, take some time to reflect on what you're looking for in a partner. It's easy to get caught up in the endless scrolling and swiping, but if you're not clear about what you want, you'll likely end up feeling overwhelmed and unsatisfied. Make a list of qualities you're looking for in a partner and stick to it. This will help you sift through profiles more efficiently and avoid wasting time on people who aren't a good fit.

While it's essential to know what you want, it's equally important to be open-minded. Remember, no one is perfect. Don't dismiss someone because they don't tick every box on your list. Instead, focus on how they make you feel. If they make you laugh, feel comfortable, and respected, these are good signs that they could be a potential match.

Another critical aspect is to manage your expectations. Online dating, like any form of dating, involves a lot of trial and error. You're not going to find 'the one' in the first few swipes. It's a process that requires patience and resilience. So, don't get discouraged if things don't work out with the first few people you meet. Remember, every failed date is a step closer to finding the right one.

Lastly, don't forget to have fun. Yes, you're on a mission to find love, but it doesn't mean you can't enjoy the journey. Make the most of your online dating experience. Take time to craft witty messages, engage in interesting conversations, and meet new people. Remember, online dating is just a tool to meet people. The real connection happens offline, so don't be afraid to take things beyond the screen when you feel ready.

In conclusion, dealing with online dating fatigue is all about balance. It's about knowing when to push forward and when to take a step back. It's about being clear about what you want, but also being open to surprises. It's about managing your expectations and remembering to have fun. And most importantly, it's about taking care of your mental health. Online dating can be a rollercoaster ride, but with the right attitude and approach, it can also lead you to the love of your life.

When to Take a Break

The art of successful Facebook dating is not just about knowing when to engage, but also when to step back. It's vital to remember that just like any other form of dating, Facebook dating too can be exhausting, and hence, taking occasional breaks can prove to be beneficial.

Now, you may wonder, why take a break? Well, for starters, it allows you to regain your perspective. Remember, the virtual world of Facebook dating can sometimes become overwhelming, creating a cycle of perpetual expectation and disappointment. This can lead to a skewed perception of reality, where you may begin to measure your self-worth based on the number of likes, comments, or responses you get. A break can help you reconnect with your real self and understand that your value is not defined by virtual interactions.

Secondly, a break can help you re-evaluate your dating strategy. If you've been on Facebook dating for a while and haven't found success, it may be time to step back and reassess. Perhaps, you're not reaching out to the right people, or maybe, your profile doesn't truly reflect who you are. A break provides you with the opportunity to reflect on these aspects and come back with a refreshed approach.

Moreover, a break can also prevent Facebook dating from becoming a chore. The initial excitement of meeting new people and exploring potential relationships can gradually fade, turning dating into a tiresome task. You may find yourself mindlessly swiping through profiles, not truly invested in the process. A break can help reignite the thrill of dating, making it an enjoyable experience once again.

But, how do you know when to take a break? There are several signs to watch out for. If you find yourself constantly checking your Facebook dating notifications, or if the first thing you do every morning is to check your messages, it may be time to take a break. Also, if you're feeling drained or disheartened by the lack of positive responses, or if you're developing negative feelings about yourself or others due to your Facebook dating experiences, these are clear indicators that you need a break.

In conclusion, taking a break from Facebook dating is not a sign of defeat, but a strategic move towards better mental health and a more effective dating approach. It allows you to step back, reassess, and re-enter the dating scene with renewed energy and perspective. So, don't hesitate to hit the pause button when you need to. After all, dating, whether in person or online, should be an enriching experience that brings joy, not stress. Embrace the journey, take breaks when needed, and remember, the right person is worth the wait.

Moving on After a Breakup

In the aftermath of a relationship's demise, the world may seem a little less bright. The hurt can be overwhelming, and picking up the pieces can seem like a daunting task. However, rising from the ashes of a broken relationship is not only possible but also an opportunity for personal growth and self-discovery. It's time to remove those rose-tinted glasses, embrace the change, and move forward.

Heartbreak is a universal experience, and social media platforms like Facebook can be a double-edged sword in these circumstances. On one hand, it can serve as a reminder of what once was, but on the other, it can be a powerful tool in your journey towards healing and new beginnings.

To start, it's crucial to resist the temptation to stalk your ex on Facebook. This behavior only prolongs the healing process by keeping you stuck in the past. Instead, utilize Facebook's "Take a Break" feature. This tool allows you to limit what you see about your ex and what they can see about you, without the finality of unfriending or blocking. It's a digital detox of sorts, giving you the space to heal without the constant reminders of your past relationship.

Next, it's time to redefine your online presence. Your Facebook profile is a reflection of who you are. Take this opportunity to update your profile picture, your interests, your activities, and your status. Let your Facebook profile be a testament to your resilience and your readiness to embrace new beginnings.

Moreover, you can use Facebook to reconnect with old friends or make new ones. Engage in groups that align with your interests, participate in discussions, and reach out to people. You'd be surprised at the support and camaraderie you can find within these virtual communities.

Furthermore, Facebook has a plethora of resources to help you navigate through this difficult time. From support groups to pages dedicated to self-help and personal growth, these resources can provide comfort, advice, and a sense of community. Remember, you're not alone in this journey.

Additionally, Facebook Dating is a feature worth exploring. It's a separate space within the Facebook app, designed to help you start meaningful relationships through things you have in common, like interests, events, and groups. It's a fresh start, a chance to meet new people and perhaps, find love again.

However, it's essential to remember that moving on doesn't mean rushing into another relationship. It's about healing, growing, and learning about yourself. It's about realizing that you're whole on your own and that another person doesn't define your worth.

In conclusion, Facebook can be a powerful ally in your journey of moving on after a breakup. It provides tools to limit contact with your ex, opportunities to redefine your online presence, resources for support and personal growth, and a platform for meeting new people. It's about using these features to your advantage, ensuring your online experience aids your healing process rather than hinders it.

So, dust off those heartbreak blues, take a deep breath, and step into this new chapter of your life with courage and optimism. Remember, every ending is a new beginning, and who knows, your next great love story might just be a Facebook notification away.

Chapter 6: Techniques for Men

Creating a Masculine Profile

In the realm of digital dating, your Facebook profile is your first impression, your handshake, your eye contact, and your pick-up line all rolled into one. It's the first and most crucial step in attracting the right person. So, how do you craft a profile that exudes masculinity, confidence, and charm?

First and foremost, let's talk about your profile picture. This is the visual representation of who you are. It's the first thing people see and it plays a big role in whether or not someone will swipe right or left. A masculine profile picture doesn't mean you need to flex your muscles or pose next to a sports car. It means you need to appear confident, approachable, and genuine. Try to choose a high-quality photo where you are smiling naturally, making eye contact with the camera, and dressed in a way that makes you feel comfortable and confident.

Next, let's move on to your 'About Me' section. This is your opportunity to show off your personality and let potential matches know what you're all about. It's important to be honest and genuine, but also to present yourself in a positive light. Avoid negativity or self-deprecation. Instead, focus on your strengths, your passions, and your ambitions. Remember, confidence is attractive and masculinity is more than just physical strength, it's also about emotional strength and self-assurance.

When writing about your hobbies and interests, be specific. Instead of just saying you like to travel, mention your favorite destinations or the most interesting place you've visited. Instead of saying you like to read, mention your favorite book or author. This not only makes your profile more interesting, but it also gives potential matches more to connect with.

Your photos and posts should also reflect your masculine energy. Share pictures of your adventures, your hobbies, or your accomplishments. But remember, it's not about showing off, it's about sharing who you are. And who you are is not just what you do, but also how you think and feel. Don't be afraid to share posts that reflect your thoughts on topics you're passionate about or your feelings about certain experiences. This will show potential matches that you're not just a man of action, but also a man of depth and introspection.

Lastly, remember that communication is key. If you receive a message or a match, respond in a timely and respectful manner. Show interest in getting to know the other person and be open to the possibility of a real connection.

Creating a masculine Facebook dating profile is not about pretending to be someone you're not. It's about presenting the best and most authentic version of yourself. It's about showing potential matches that you're confident, interesting, and genuinely interested in making a connection. So, put some thought into your profile, be honest, be confident, and most importantly, be yourself. After all, the most attractive thing a man can be is comfortable in his own skin.

First Message Techniques for Men

Navigating the world of Facebook dating can be a daunting task for many men. However, the key to successfully connecting with potential partners lies in the art of crafting a compelling first message. This chapter will arm you with the knowledge to make that first impression count and increase your chances of success.

The first message you send on Facebook Dating is akin to a first impression in real life. It sets the tone for your interaction and can be the difference between a fruitful conversation and a missed connection. Your message should be unique, thoughtful, and personalized. Generic messages such as "hey" or "how's it going" often go unnoticed in a sea of similar messages. It's crucial to stand out from the crowd and show genuine interest in the person you're messaging.

Start by thoroughly reading the person's profile. This can give you valuable insight into their interests, hobbies, and personality. Use this information to craft a message that not only shows you've taken the time to get to know them but also sparks a conversation. For example, if they mention a love for hiking, you could ask about their favorite trails or share a hiking experience of your own.

Humor can also be a powerful tool in your first message. A well-placed joke or witty remark can break the ice and make your message more memorable. However, ensure your humor is respectful and not at the expense of the person you're messaging. The goal is to make them smile, not offend them.

Additionally, it's crucial to keep your first message concise. A lengthy message can be overwhelming and might deter the person from responding. Aim for a few sentences that express your interest and ignite a conversation. Remember, the goal of the first message isn't to bare your soul but to pique their interest and encourage a response.

It's also important to be patient. Not everyone checks their messages regularly, and it may take some time to receive a response. Don't be disheartened if you don't get an immediate reply. Avoid sending multiple messages as this can come across as desperate and might discourage the person from responding.

Lastly, always maintain respect and consideration in your messaging. Avoid overly sexual or offensive language, and never pressure someone into responding. Everyone on Facebook Dating is there to make connections, and showing respect for that process will only increase your chances of success.

Remember, crafting a compelling first message is an art, not a science. It may take some practice to find what works best for you. But by following these guidelines, you'll be well on your way to making meaningful connections on Facebook Dating.

In conclusion, the first message can make or break your chances of success on Facebook Dating. It should be unique, thoughtful, and personalized, showing genuine interest in the person you're messaging. With patience, respect, and a dash of humor, you can craft a first message that stands out from the crowd and paves the way for a fruitful conversation.

Keeping Her Interested

The allure of the chase is often more enticing than the catch itself. This philosophy is especially true when it comes to dating in the digital age. It's not enough to catch her attention; the real challenge lies in keeping her interested. Here's how to do just that on Facebook Dating.

Firstly, consistency is key. Consistency in your communication shows that you are genuinely interested in her. Engage with her posts, react to her stories, and slide into her inbox with thoughtful messages, but avoid coming off as too desperate or too available. Your goal is to pique her curiosity, not to smother her.

Secondly, remember that women appreciate men who take the time to get to know them. Use Facebook's 'About' section to your advantage. Find out her interests, hobbies, favorite books, or movies. Use this information to start meaningful conversations. Show her that you're interested in more than just her profile picture. This will make her feel valued and appreciated.

Thirdly, be original and authentic. Women are smart; they can tell when you're trying too hard or being fake. Avoid generic compliments and clichéd pick-up lines. Instead, pay attention to her posts and pictures and compliment her on something specific. This demonstrates that you're paying attention and that you appreciate her for who she is, not just for her looks.

Fourthly, keep things fun and interesting. The digital world can be monotonous, and it's easy for conversations to become routine and boring. Break the monotony by sharing interesting articles, funny memes, or engaging videos. This will not only keep the conversation lively but also show her that you have a sense of humor.

Lastly, remember that patience is a virtue. Women don't like to feel rushed or pressured into anything. Take your time getting to know her. Show her that you're interested in building a genuine connection, not just a quick fling. This will make her feel comfortable and more likely to open up to you.

In conclusion, keeping her interested on Facebook Dating is not about playing games or pretending to be someone you're not. It's about being genuine, consistent, and patient. It's about showing her that you value her as a person, that you're interested in getting to know her, and that you're willing to put in the effort to do so.

So, take a deep breath, put on your best digital charm, and dive into the exciting world of Facebook Dating. Remember, the goal is not just to catch her attention but to keep her interested. With these tips, you're well on your way to doing just that. Happy dating!

Handling Rejection

The world of Facebook dating is not always a bed of roses. Sometimes, the road to finding your perfect match can be paved with a lot of heartache and rejection. However, it is crucial to remember that rejection is a normal part of the dating process. It is not a reflection of your worth, but rather a sign that the person you were interested in was not the right match for you.

The first step to handling rejection is to understand that it is not personal. When someone rejects you, it is not because there is something wrong with you. Rather, it is because they did not see the potential for a relationship with you. This could be due to a variety of reasons, such as not being ready for a relationship, having different life goals, or simply not feeling a connection. It is crucial to remember that everyone has different tastes and preferences, and just because one person does not see your worth does not mean that others will not.

When faced with rejection, it is important not to let it affect your self-esteem. You are still the same amazing person you were before the rejection, and someone else's inability to see that does not change it. Instead of dwelling on the rejection, use it as an opportunity to learn and grow. Reflect on the experience and think about what you can do differently next time. Perhaps you came on too strong, or maybe you did not express your feelings clearly enough.

Whatever the case, use the rejection as a learning experience to improve your future dating endeavors.

One of the biggest mistakes people make when facing rejection is to isolate themselves. It is natural to want to retreat and lick your wounds, but it is crucial to stay connected with your friends and loved ones. They can provide the support and perspective you need to move past the rejection. Moreover, maintaining an active social life can help you meet new people and potentially find a better match.

Another critical aspect of handling rejection is to stay positive. It can be easy to fall into a negative mindset and start doubting your self-worth, but this will only hinder your chances of finding love. Instead, try to stay positive and keep your chin up. Remember, every rejection is just one step closer to finding the right person for you.

Lastly, do not let rejection deter you from continuing to put yourself out there. It can be tempting to close yourself off after a rejection, but this will only prevent you from finding love. Instead, keep trying and keep putting yourself out there. Remember, the right person might be just around the corner, and you will never meet them if you give up.

In conclusion, rejection is a normal part of the dating process and is not a reflection of your worth. By understanding this, maintaining your self-esteem, staying connected with friends, staying positive, and continuing to put yourself out there, you can handle rejection and continue on your journey to finding love on Facebook.

Moving from Online to Offline

In the world of digital dating, making a connection goes beyond the borders of the virtual realm. The true essence of a relationship is best felt in person, where you can touch, feel, and experience your partner's presence. Facebook Dating is a fantastic platform to meet your potential partner, but the real magic happens when you take your relationship offline.

You've already made the first move by setting up your Facebook Dating profile, and you've started engaging with potential matches. You've sent messages back and forth, and you've felt a connection. Now, it's time to take the next big step - moving from online to offline.

Taking your online relationship offline can be a daunting task. It's a significant shift from the comfort of your smartphone screen to the unpredictable real world. But, it's a step that is essential if you want to build a real, meaningful relationship. It's about taking a leap of faith, stepping outside your comfort zone, and allowing yourself to experience the thrill of a real-life connection.

When you meet in person, you have the opportunity to create shared experiences, which are the building blocks of any strong relationship. These experiences, whether they're simple things like watching a movie together or going on a vacation, enable you to understand your partner better. They help you discover their likes, dislikes, quirks, and passions. This understanding is what ultimately leads to a deep and meaningful connection.

However, moving from online to offline requires careful thought and planning. It's not about rushing into a meeting. It's about creating a safe and comfortable space for both you and your potential partner. Always choose a public place for your first meeting and tell a friend or family member about your plans.

Remember, the goal here is not to impress but to express. It's not about putting on a show or pretending to be someone you're not. It's about being genuine and authentic.

It's about showing your potential partner the real you. After all, the foundation of any lasting relationship is honesty and authenticity.

Also, keep in mind that it's okay to feel nervous. It's natural to have butterflies in your stomach. But don't let the nerves get the best of you. Take deep breaths, relax, and remember that it's just a meeting. It's an opportunity for you to get to know your potential partner better.

In conclusion, moving from online to offline is an exciting journey. It's a journey that requires courage, patience, and a lot of understanding. But, it's a journey that's worth every step. It's a journey that could lead you to the love of your life. So, take the plunge, make the move, and enjoy the thrilling journey of offline dating. Because, in the end, it's not about how you met, but how you connect.

Remember, Facebook Dating is just a tool to meet potential partners. It's the first step in the dating process. The real relationship begins when you take it offline. So, don't hesitate. Take the leap, and let the magic of real-life dating unfold.

Chapter 7: Techniques for Women

Creating a Feminine Profile

In the world of online dating, first impressions are critically important, and it all begins with your profile. If you are a woman looking to attract the right kind of attention, it is essential to create a feminine profile that reflects your personality, interests, and what you are looking for in a partner.

Crafting a feminine profile is not about projecting a false image or pretending to be someone you're not. It's about highlighting your unique qualities in a way that appeals to the opposite sex. You don't need to pretend to be the "perfect woman". Instead, be genuine, be you, but be the best version of you.

To start, choose a profile picture that best represents you. This should be a clear, high-quality image that shows off your natural beauty. Avoid using filters or editing tools that drastically alter your appearance. Remember, the goal is to attract a partner who appreciates you for who you are, not for a digitally enhanced version of yourself. Your profile picture should make you look approachable, so a warm smile is always a good idea.

The next step is to write a compelling bio. This is your opportunity to showcase your personality and interests. Avoid generic phrases and clichés such as "I love to laugh" or "I enjoy long walks on the beach." Instead, share specific details about your hobbies, passions, and goals. For example, instead of saying "I love music," you could say "I'm a classically trained pianist who also enjoys attending live rock concerts." This not only makes your profile more interesting, but it also gives potential matches more to connect with.

It's also important to convey what kind of relationship you're seeking. If you're looking for a serious relationship, state it. If you're interested in casual dating, be clear about it. This will help filter out incompatible matches and attract those who are looking for the same thing as you.

Finally, maintain a positive tone. While it's important to be honest, avoid focusing on negative experiences or what you don't want in a partner. Instead, emphasize what you do want and what you're excited about in a potential match.

This will make your profile more inviting and attractive to potential partners.

Also, don't forget to update your profile regularly. This not only shows that you are active on the platform but also gives potential matches new things to learn about you. Whether it's a new hobby you've picked up, a book you've recently read, or a trip you've taken, sharing these updates can spark interesting conversations and deepen connections.

In conclusion, creating a feminine profile on Facebook Dating is about presenting a genuine, appealing snapshot of who you are. It's about showcasing your unique qualities, expressing your desires in a partner, and maintaining a positive, inviting tone. By following these guidelines, you can create a profile that not only attracts the right kind of attention but also sets the stage for meaningful connections.

First Message Techniques for Women

Ladies, it's time to take control of your love life. Rather than sitting back and waiting for someone to approach you, why not make the first move? Just as in the physical world, the digital realm of Facebook dating is an open playing field where you can take the lead. The key is to understand how to initiate a conversation that leaves a lasting impression. To help you do just that, we've compiled some effective first message techniques for women.

The first crucial step is to make your message personalized. Gone are the days when a generic "Hey" or "Hi" would suffice. The modern man appreciates a woman who takes the time to read his profile and highlight something specific that caught her attention. Maybe he has a picture of himself hiking and you love the outdoors, or perhaps he mentions his passion for cooking and you're a foodie too. Use these shared interests as a conversation starter. Not only will this show that you've taken an interest in him as an individual, but it will also provide a common ground to build upon.

Secondly, pose a question in your first message. Why? Because questions demand answers. A well-placed question encourages a response and keeps the conversation flowing. However, the key is to ask open-ended questions rather than ones that require a simple 'yes' or 'no'. For example, if he's a fan of a particular band, instead of asking "Do you like [band's name]?", you could ask "What's your favorite [band's name] song and why?" This will give him more to respond to and show that you're genuinely interested in his likes and opinions.

Humor is another great weapon in your messaging arsenal. A good laugh can break the ice and make the conversation a lot more enjoyable. If you share a funny anecdote or make a light-hearted joke about something in his profile, it can add a spark to your conversation. But remember, humor is subjective and should be used wisely. Always keep it positive and avoid anything that could potentially be offensive.

Compliments, when used judiciously, can also work wonders. Everyone likes to feel appreciated and a genuine compliment can go a long way in making a person feel special. However, try to steer clear of cliched compliments about looks. Instead, compliment him on something unique to his profile - his taste in music, his sense of style, or his adventurous spirit.

Finally, keep your first message short and sweet. While it's important to show interest, you don't want to come across as desperate or overbearing. A few well-crafted sentences are more than enough to pique his interest and encourage a response.

Remember, the goal of the first message is not to seal the deal, but to open a door. It's an opportunity to show your interest, reveal a bit of your personality, and invite a response. So, ladies, it's time to take the reins, step out of your comfort zone, and make the first move with confidence. After all, in the world of Facebook dating, you're just a message away from potentially meeting the love of your life.

Keeping Him Interested

Once you've successfully caught his attention on Facebook, the real challenge begins. Keeping him interested is the key to transforming a simple Facebook connection into a potential romantic relationship. In the digital age, it's easy to get lost in the crowd. However, with the right strategies, you can stand out and maintain his interest.

First and foremost, always be yourself. Authenticity is attractive and it's crucial to build any relationship on a foundation of honesty. Don't pretend to be someone you're not just to keep his attention. If he's genuinely interested in you, he will appreciate your originality and uniqueness.

Next, be active and engaging on your Facebook profile. Share posts that reflect your personality, interests, and life experiences. Your posts should give him a glimpse into your world, sparking his curiosity and prompting him to want to know more about you. However, remember to maintain a balance; you don't want to flood his newsfeed and risk coming across as desperate or obsessive.

Engage him in conversation. Encourage him to share his thoughts, opinions, and experiences. This will not only keep him interested but also help you to understand him better. Show genuine interest in what he says. React to his posts, comment on them, and share your own insights. This will show him that you're not only interested in him but also value his thoughts and opinions.

Be patient and don't rush things. Building a meaningful relationship takes time. Don't push him to commit or rush into a relationship. Let things unfold naturally. If he feels pressured, he might pull back.

Show him that you have a life outside of Facebook. While it's important to stay connected on the platform, it's equally important to show him that you have a fulfilling life offline. Share pictures of your adventures, hobbies, or anything that you're passionate about. This will not only make you more attractive but also show him that you're not overly dependent on him for your happiness.

Remember, everyone loves a good mystery. So, keep a little mystery about yourself. Don't reveal everything about you at once. Let him discover more about you gradually. This will keep him intrigued and wanting to know more.

Lastly, be positive and fun. Nobody likes to be around negative or boring people. Make sure your posts and messages are upbeat and full of positivity. Show him that you're someone who knows how to enjoy life.

Keeping him interested is not about playing games or manipulating his feelings. It's about showing him the real you, engaging him in meaningful conversations, and giving him a reason to want to know more about you. When you do this, you're not just keeping his interest, you're also building a strong foundation for a potential relationship.

Remember, Facebook is just a tool to connect with people. The real magic happens when you take the relationship off the screen and into the real world. So, use these strategies to keep him interested on Facebook, but always aim to move the relationship beyond the digital world.

Handling Rejection

It's inevitable. Not every person you approach or interact with on Facebook Dating will be interested. You may face rejection, and that's perfectly okay. It's an integral part of the dating process. The key lies in how you handle it.

Firstly, it's essential to remember that rejection is not a reflection of your self-worth. Every individual has their own unique tastes and preferences. Just because one person isn't interested doesn't mean that you're unattractive or undesirable. It merely means that this particular person did not see a potential match. There are plenty of other users on Facebook Dating who might find you intriguing.

Embrace rejection as an opportunity for growth and self-improvement. It can be a valuable source of feedback. If someone says no, ask yourself why that might be. Are you coming on too strong? Is your profile not accurately representing who you are? Instead of seeing rejection as a failure, see it as a chance to sharpen your social skills and improve your online dating game.

Moreover, do not let rejection discourage you. It's easy to feel disheartened and want to give up, but persistence is key. Remember, finding the right match often takes time, and everyone faces rejection at some point or another. It's a part of the journey.

When faced with rejection, maintain your dignity and respect the other person's decision. Respond politely and move on. It's not about winning or losing; it's about finding someone compatible. If they're not interested, they're simply not the right fit for you. There's no need to convince them otherwise or take it personally.

It's also crucial to maintain a positive attitude. Rejection can be a blow to your self-esteem, but don't let it dampen your spirits. Keep in mind that everyone has different tastes, and just because one person wasn't interested doesn't mean others won't be. Stay positive and keep putting yourself out there.

Finally, use rejection as a motivator. Let it fuel your determination to find the right match. If you've been rejected, that means you're trying. You're putting yourself out there and taking risks, which is something to be proud of. Each rejection brings you one step closer to finding the right match.

In conclusion, handling rejection is all about perspective. It's not a failure but a stepping stone towards finding the right person. It's an opportunity for growth, improvement, and resilience. Remember, it's not about how many times you're knocked down but how many times you get back up. So, the next time you face rejection on Facebook Dating, take it in stride. Learn from it, grow from it, and let it propel you forward. Your ideal match could be just around the corner.

Moving from Online to Offline

Once you've successfully navigated the online world of Facebook dating, the time will come to translate your digital connection into a real-life encounter. This is a crucial step, one that requires careful consideration and planning. It's a transition that can be fraught with anxiety, but with the right preparation, it can also be an exhilarating leap into a new phase of your relationship.

The first thing to remember is that the context of your online interactions will be different from your offline encounters. The charm and wit that you've so carefully crafted in your Facebook messages might not translate as smoothly in person. Therefore, it's essential to be genuine

101

and authentic from the very beginning, both online and offline.

When you decide to meet in person, be sure to choose a neutral and public location for your first date. This not only ensures your safety but also helps to alleviate some of the pressure. Meeting in a familiar place where you both feel comfortable will help the conversation flow more naturally and make the meeting less intimidating.

Next, it's important to manage expectations. Remember that the person you've been chatting with online might not be exactly the same in person. This isn't necessarily a bad thing - it's just a part of getting to know someone in a more intimate and nuanced way. Don't let any initial awkwardness deter you. It's perfectly normal and a part of the dating process.

One of the most important things to remember when moving from online to offline is to be patient. It might take some time to build the same level of comfort and intimacy that you had online. Don't rush things. Allow your relationship to develop at its own pace.

Also, remember to keep communication open and honest. If you feel uncomfortable or uncertain at any point, express this to your partner. Honesty is a vital part of any relationship, and it's especially important when transitioning from an online to an offline relationship.

Make an effort to keep the conversation light and fun during your first few dates. This will help both of you feel more comfortable and will make the transition from online to offline smoother. Share stories, laugh, and enjoy each other's company. This is your chance to build a stronger connection, so make the most of it.

Finally, remember to have fun. Dating should be an enjoyable experience, not a stressful chore. Keep an open mind, be yourself, and enjoy the process of getting to know each other in a new and exciting way.

In conclusion, moving from online to offline dating can be a thrilling journey. It's an opportunity to deepen your connection and explore the potential of your relationship. By being genuine, managing expectations, keeping communication open, and maintaining a patient and positive attitude, you can successfully navigate this transition and create a meaningful relationship that started on Facebook.

So, are you ready to take the leap from online to offline? Trust in your connection and in the strength of the bond you've built online. With the right approach, you'll find that the journey from online to offline dating is not only manageable but also truly rewarding.

Chapter 8: Dating Etiquette

Being Authentic

When it comes to the world of Facebook dating, one crucial secret you must grasp is the power of authenticity. It's easy to hide behind a carefully crafted persona, especially in the digital world, but such facades can only take you so far. Authenticity, being your true self, is the key to making meaningful connections and finding genuine love online.

In the realm of Facebook dating, authenticity is a currency. It's a means of establishing trust, fostering intimacy, and building a strong foundation for a lasting relationship. People are drawn to authenticity because it's rare and valuable, particularly in the world of online dating where pretense and exaggeration are common.

Think about it this way: Would you prefer to connect with someone who presents a polished, but possibly false, image of themselves, or would you rather engage with someone who is unapologetically themselves, flaws and all? Most people gravitate towards the latter. Why? Because authenticity breeds trust, and trust is the cornerstone of any successful relationship.

Being authentic on Facebook dating doesn't mean revealing every single detail about your life from the get-go. It means being honest about who you are, what you want, and what you value. It means presenting yourself truthfully, from your profile picture to your personal interests and life goals. It's about consistency between your words and actions, your online persona, and your offline reality.

Think of your authenticity as your personal brand. It's what sets you apart from the crowd and makes you uniquely you. It's your secret weapon in the competitive world of online dating. And just like a brand, authenticity takes time to build and maintain, but the rewards are well worth the effort.

So, how do you project authenticity on Facebook dating? Start by being honest in your profile. Choose a profile picture that genuinely represents you, not an overly edited or outdated photo. When describing yourself, avoid clichés and generic descriptions. Instead, share your unique interests, passions, and quirks. Remember, it's your uniqueness that makes you attractive.

When interacting with potential matches, be genuine in your communication. Don't pretend to be someone you're not just to impress or fit in. It might work in the short term, but in the end, it's exhausting and unsustainable. Instead, express your true thoughts and feelings, even if they're not always what the other person wants to hear. Authenticity might be risky, but it's also liberating and attractive.

Remember, being authentic doesn't mean you have to be perfect. In fact, it's the opposite. Authenticity is about embracing your imperfections and vulnerabilities. It's about showing that you're human, just like everyone else. It's about proving that you're real, not just another profile on a screen.

In conclusion, authenticity is the secret sauce that can make your Facebook dating experience successful and fulfilling. It's the key to attracting the right people, building meaningful relationships, and ultimately, finding genuine love online. So, dare to be authentic, dare to be you. Your future partner will thank you for it.

Respecting Boundaries

In the world of Facebook dating, one crucial aspect that cannot be overlooked is the importance of respecting boundaries. This goes beyond just understanding when it's appropriate to send a friend request or a private message; it's about acknowledging and respecting the personal space and privacy of the person you're interested in.

It's essential to remember that everyone has their own comfort level when it comes to how much they share online. Some people are very open and post frequently about their personal lives, while others are more reserved and prefer to keep certain aspects of their lives private. It's crucial to respect these differences and not to push someone to share more than they're comfortable with.

For instance, if the person you're interested in doesn't post many personal photos or updates, it's generally a good idea to refrain from asking them to do so. This could come across as invasive and could potentially make them feel uncomfortable. Instead, take the time to get to know them on their terms. Engage with their posts in a respectful and genuine manner, and let them decide when and how they want to share more personal aspects of their lives.

Similarly, it's important to respect their time and attention. Just because someone is active on Facebook doesn't mean they're available for a chat at all times. Don't bombard them with messages or expect immediate responses. Recognize that they have a life outside of Facebook and respect their time.

Moreover, refrain from over-commenting or liking every single post they make. While it's important to show interest and engage with their content, doing so excessively can come off as creepy or desperate. Instead, be selective with your interactions and ensure they are meaningful and genuine.

When it comes to Facebook dating, it's also crucial to respect the other person's boundaries when it comes to the relationship's progression. Just because you're ready to change your relationship status or share couple photos doesn't mean they are. Always discuss these decisions with the other person and ensure they're comfortable with them before proceeding.

In essence, the key to successful Facebook dating lies in respecting boundaries. It's about recognizing and appreciating the other person's comfort levels and privacy, and not pushing them to share more than they're willing to. By doing so, you'll not only show them that you respect them as an individual, but you'll also create a stronger foundation for your potential relationship.

Remember, every successful relationship is built on mutual respect and understanding. In the world of Facebook dating, this begins with respecting boundaries. So, take the time to understand the other person's comfort levels, respect their privacy, and engage with them on their terms. Not only will this make you more appealing, but it'll also increase your chances of forming a meaningful and lasting connection.

In conclusion, respect is the cornerstone of any relationship, including those formed on Facebook. By respecting boundaries, you're showing the other person that you value their comfort and privacy. This will not only make your interactions more enjoyable, but it will also set the stage for a potential relationship built on mutual respect and understanding.

Handling Disagreements

In the fascinating world of Facebook dating, one must always be prepared to navigate the unpredictable waters of disagreements. As we venture into this realm, it's crucial to understand that disagreements are a natural part of any relationship, even those that begin online. Instead of perceiving these instances as a threat, we should see them as opportunities to deepen our understanding of our partner and enrich our relationship.

In the midst of a disagreement, it's easy to get caught up in the heat of the moment and lose sight of the bigger picture. But remember, every conflict is a chance to learn more about your partner's thoughts, feelings, and perspectives. It's an opportunity to improve your communication skills, which are vital in any relationship.

Firstly, when a disagreement arises, it's essential to approach it with an open mind. Instead of stubbornly sticking to your viewpoint, try to understand the other person's perspective. This doesn't mean you have to agree with them, but showing empathy can significantly diffuse tension. Remember, it's not about winning or losing; it's about reaching a mutual understanding.

Secondly, maintain respect throughout the disagreement. Even if you're upset, it's crucial to avoid disrespectful language or actions. Remember, you're dealing with a person who has feelings just like you. Treat them with the same respect you'd want in return. This approach not only helps to maintain a healthy relationship but also promotes a positive communication environment.

Thirdly, communicate effectively. This involves expressing your feelings and thoughts clearly and honestly, but also listening actively to your partner. Effective communication is a two-way street. It's not just about getting your point across, but also understanding your partner's viewpoint.

Another crucial aspect of handling disagreements is not letting them linger. It's easy to ignore a problem and hope it goes away on its own. But unresolved issues can fester and lead to bigger problems down the line. So, address disagreements as soon as they arise. It might be uncomfortable, but it's necessary for the health of your relationship.

Finally, don't be afraid to apologize when you're wrong. Pride can often get in the way of resolving disagreements, but admitting when you're wrong shows maturity and respect for your partner. It also provides an opportunity for growth and learning, which can strengthen your relationship in the long run.

Disagreements can be challenging, but they don't have to be destructive. With the right approach, they can be constructive and lead to a stronger, more understanding relationship. So, when you find yourself in the throes of a disagreement, remember these tips. Approach the situation with an open mind, maintain respect, communicate effectively, address issues promptly, and don't hesitate to apologize when necessary.

In the world of Facebook dating, disagreements are inevitable. But with the right approach, they can be navigated successfully. So, embrace them as a natural part of your online dating journey, and use them as opportunities to deepen your relationship and enhance your communication skills.

When to Meet in Person

As you navigate the exciting world of Facebook dating, one question that is sure to arise is, "When is the right time to meet in person?" Understanding the perfect timing for this crucial step can make all the difference in creating a successful connection. This chapter offers you insights into making this decision wisely and effectively.

First off, it's essential to note that there is no one-size-fits-all answer to this question. The timing of your first in-person meeting should be dictated by your comfort level, the quality of your online interactions, and your mutual agreement. However, certain pointers can guide you in this process.

The beauty of Facebook dating is that it allows you to develop a connection and build rapport with someone before deciding to meet in person. You can explore each other's interests, values, and aspirations, understand each other's lifestyles, and even gauge each other's sense of humor. This process allows you to assess your compatibility without the pressure of a face-to-face meeting.

However, it's also important to remember that online interactions have their limitations. They can sometimes create an idealized image of the other person, which may not align with reality. Therefore, it's advisable to meet in person when you feel you've established a good online connection but before you're too emotionally invested. This meeting can help you confirm whether the chemistry you feel online translates into real life.

The safety aspect is another crucial consideration. While Facebook dating offers various safety features, meeting someone from the internet always carries a certain level of risk. Therefore, before deciding to meet in person, make sure you feel safe and secure. Trust your instincts. If something feels off, take your time or choose not to meet at all.

When you both feel ready to meet, plan your first date in a public place, during daylight hours, and let someone know where you're going and who you're meeting. This is not just about physical safety, but also about emotional comfort. Meeting in a familiar, public place can ease the pressure and make the experience more enjoyable.

Conversely, rushing into an in-person meeting can lead to awkwardness or disappointment. If you meet too early, without having a sense of who the other person is, you may find that you have little in common or that the physical chemistry you hoped for simply isn't there. So, take your time to get to know each other online first.

In conclusion, the right time to meet in person while Facebook dating varies from one person to another. It's a balance between not waiting too long and not rushing in prematurely. It's about ensuring safety, comfort, and a reasonable level of compatibility before taking the relationship offline. Remember, Facebook dating is not about racing to the finish line; it's about enjoying the journey and making meaningful connections along the way. So, trust your instincts, communicate openly, and take the step to meet in person when it feels right.

Breakup Etiquette

In the realm of Facebook dating, the end of a relationship can be a delicate matter. It's not just about the emotional fallout; it's also about how you handle your digital footprint. Just as there are rules for how to behave during a date, there are also protocols to follow when it comes to the aftermath of a breakup. This chapter will guide you through the labyrinth of 'Breakup Etiquette' in the context of Facebook dating.

When a relationship ends, it's crucial to be respectful. Even if things ended on a sour note, it's important to remember that at one point, you shared something special. Airing your
116

dirty laundry on Facebook can be tempting, especially in the heat of the moment. However, it's crucial to keep your emotions in check and avoid posting anything that you might regret later. Maintaining dignity and respect, both for yourself and your ex, is the hallmark of a mature individual.

Unfriending or blocking your ex right after a breakup might seem like a good idea, but it's generally better to avoid such drastic steps. It's more respectful to have a conversation about your online boundaries. If you both agree to limit your online interaction, it can make the transition easier. However, if seeing their posts causes you pain, it might be best to unfollow them temporarily. This way, their posts won't appear in your news feed, but you won't completely cut them out of your life.

When it comes to changing your relationship status, timing is everything. Doing it too soon might seem insensitive, while waiting too long could give false hope. It's best to discuss this with your ex and decide on a suitable timeline. When you do change your status, avoid adding a dramatic or hurtful comment. Remember, the goal is to handle the breakup with grace and dignity.

If you've shared pictures or posts with your ex, you might be tempted to delete them. However, consider that these posts are part of your digital history. Instead of erasing them completely, you could adjust the privacy settings so that they're only visible to you. This way, you're not erasing your past, but you're also not flaunting it.

Breakups are hard, and it's natural to seek support from friends. However, refrain from rallying your friends against your ex. It's unfair to put them in the middle of your breakup. Instead, seek support offline or in private messages.

Lastly, resist the urge to stalk your ex's profile. It's natural to be curious about what they're up to, but this can lead to obsessive behavior and prevent you from moving on. Instead, focus on your own healing and growth.

In conclusion, navigating the digital aftermath of a breakup can be tricky, but with a little bit of grace and a lot of respect, it's possible to handle it in a way that preserves your dignity and respects your ex's feelings. Remember, just because the relationship ended doesn't mean you have to end on bad terms.

Chapter 9: Overcoming Common Challenges

Dealing with Fake Profiles

In the fascinating world of Facebook dating, one of the first obstacles you may encounter is the presence of fake profiles. These are profiles created with false information or stolen identities, primarily designed to deceive and manipulate. It's vital to recognize, understand, and deal with these profiles effectively, as they can pose a significant threat to your online dating experience.

Fake profiles are not only a nuisance but also a potential danger. They can lead to emotional distress, financial loss, and in some cases, even identity theft. So, how can you protect yourself from these digital wolves in sheep's clothing? The key lies in awareness, vigilance, and caution.

Firstly, be aware that fake profiles exist. They are more common than you might think. In fact, Facebook itself estimates that about 5% of its active accounts are fake. This may not seem like a significant figure, but when you consider Facebook's colossal user base, it translates to millions of fake profiles.

Next, be vigilant. Pay close attention to the details of the profiles you interact with. Fake profiles often have certain tell-tale signs. These might include a lack of personal information, only one or two pictures, or photos that look like they've been taken from a magazine or stock image site. Additionally, they might send you messages that are overly flattering, vague, or filled with grammatical and spelling errors. If a profile exhibits several of these signs, it's likely fake.

However, it's crucial to remember that not all fake profiles are obvious. Some are sophisticated and well-crafted, designed to convincingly mimic real people. That's why it's essential to proceed with caution. Don't give out personal or financial information to anyone you've just met online, no matter how genuine they seem. Keep your interactions on the platform until you've built a level of trust and have confirmed the person's identity through other means.

If you suspect a profile is fake, report it. Facebook has mechanisms in place to deal with fake profiles, and your report can help keep the community safer. Furthermore, don't be afraid to cut off communication if something feels off. Trust your instincts. It's better to be safe than sorry.

In conclusion, while fake profiles are a real problem in the world of Facebook dating, they don't have to ruin your experience. By being aware, vigilant, and cautious, you can protect yourself and enjoy the exciting journey of finding love online. Remember, genuine people are out there, so don't let the fakes discourage you.

So, equip yourself with these tips, and dive into the thrilling world of Facebook dating. After all, amidst the sea of profiles, your perfect match could be just a click away. Don't let the fear of fake profiles deter you from your quest for love. Instead, use it as a tool to navigate the waters with wisdom and caution. Because in the end, the reward of finding genuine connection far outweighs the risks.

Handling Online Harassment

As you navigate the exciting world of Facebook Dating, it's important to be aware of a less pleasant aspect of online interaction: harassment. It's unfortunate, but the digital sphere is not free from this negative behavior. However, equipped with the right knowledge and tools, you can handle online harassment effectively and continue your journey towards finding your perfect match.

Firstly, let's define what online harassment is. It can range from unsolicited messages, offensive comments, or even threatening behavior. It's crucial to remember that nobody deserves to be treated this way, and it's not your fault if you become a target. The anonymity of the internet sometimes emboldens individuals to behave poorly.

So, how do you handle online harassment? Firstly, don't engage with the harasser. Responding to their provocations is feeding into their desire for attention or control. Instead, make use of Facebook's features designed to protect you. Block the individual in question. This prevents them from seeing your profile, interacting with your posts, or contacting you.

Next, report the incident to Facebook. The platform has a responsibility to maintain a safe and respectful environment for its users. Include screenshots and other evidence in your report. Facebook takes these matters seriously and can take action such as suspending or banning the offender.

Remember, you're not alone in this situation. Reach out to your friends or family for support. They can provide comfort, advice, and even back you up by reporting the harasser. If the harassment escalates or becomes threatening, don't hesitate to contact your local authorities. Online harassment can be a form of cybercrime, and law enforcement can intervene.

Don't let the fear of harassment deter you from your online dating journey. Instead, use it as an opportunity to set clear boundaries and expectations. Be clear about the kind of interaction you are comfortable with, and don't be afraid to assert yourself when these boundaries are crossed.

Privacy settings are your friend. Use them to control who can see your posts, photos, and personal information. This can minimize unsolicited attention and potential harassment.

Consider joining groups or communities on Facebook where respectful interaction is enforced. These can be a great place to meet like-minded individuals.

Maintaining a positive mindset is also key. For every individual who chooses to behave poorly, there are many more who are respectful and genuine. Don't let the actions of a few color your entire online dating experience.

Lastly, practice self-care. If an incident of harassment has left you feeling upset or anxious, take a break from Facebook Dating. Engage in activities that you enjoy and that make you feel good about yourself. This can help you regain a sense of control and positivity.

Online harassment is a regrettable reality of the digital age, but you have the tools and the power to handle it effectively. Don't let it discourage you from your pursuit of love. Remember, your safety and well-being are paramount, and you deserve to enjoy your online dating experience free from harassment. With a combination of vigilance, assertiveness, and the right use of Facebook's protective features, you can navigate Facebook Dating confidently and securely.

Navigating Long Distance Relationships

In the realm of Facebook dating, one of the most challenging aspects you might encounter is managing long-distance relationships. It's no secret that long-distance relationships come with their own unique set of challenges, but with the right approach, they can be navigated successfully.

The first step in successfully navigating a long-distance relationship on Facebook dating is communication. Communication is the lifeblood of any relationship, but it becomes even more crucial when distance is involved. With the array of communication features that Facebook offers, keeping in touch with your partner should never be a problem. Use Facebook Messenger for regular chats, send voice notes when you miss hearing each other's voices, and make video calls to create a sense of closeness. By utilizing these features, you can maintain a strong connection with your partner, regardless of the miles separating you.

The second step involves setting shared goals. A long-distance relationship without a shared vision can feel like a ship lost at sea. Discussing your future plans together and setting common goals can give your relationship direction and purpose. It can also help to alleviate the uncertainties and insecurities that often accompany long-distance relationships.

Next, trust is paramount. This may seem obvious, but it's worth emphasizing. Long-distance relationships require a high level of trust since you can't be together physically all the time. You must trust that your partner is being faithful and honest with you, just as they must trust you. Facebook can be a double-edged sword in this regard. On the one hand, it can provide reassurance through constant communication, but on the other hand, it can breed insecurity if misused. So, use Facebook to build trust, not break it.

Another critical aspect of long-distance relationships is finding ways to spend quality time together, despite the distance. With Facebook's various features, you can watch movies together, play games, or even go on virtual dates. These shared experiences can help to strengthen your bond and keep the spark alive in your relationship.

Lastly, patience is a virtue that you'll need in abundance. Long-distance relationships are a marathon, not a sprint. It may take time to adjust to the distance and the unique challenges it presents. But with patience and perseverance, you can make it work.

In conclusion, navigating a long-distance relationship on Facebook dating is not an easy task. It requires commitment, effort, and a good dose of creativity. But with the right approach, it's entirely possible to maintain a healthy and fulfilling relationship, despite the miles in between. So, don't let distance deter you. Embrace the challenge, and use the tips provided to make your long-distance relationship a success. Remember, love knows no boundaries, not even those of distance.

Overcoming Language Barriers

The art of communication is a delicate dance that takes two to tango. In the realm of Facebook dating, language often takes center stage, acting as the bridge that connects two hearts. However, language barriers can be a stumbling block that can turn this dance into a clumsy tumble. But fear not! Language barriers are not insurmountable obstacles, rather they are challenges that can be conquered with the right strategies.

First and foremost, let's address the elephant in the room. Yes, language barriers can be daunting. But remember, every challenge is an opportunity in disguise. In the context of Facebook dating, language barriers can actually be a catalyst that sparks unique and memorable conversations. After all, who could forget the charming exchange where you both tried to teach each other words from your native tongues? These moments of shared laughter and learning can lay the foundation for a lasting bond.

Now, let's delve into some effective strategies to overcome language barriers. One of the best ways to bridge this gap is by using translation tools. Facebook Messenger, the platform where most of your conversations will take place, has a built-in translation feature. This can be a lifesaver in many situations. However, keep in mind that translation tools are not flawless. Sometimes, they can misinterpret the nuances of a language, leading to confusion. Thus, it's crucial to maintain a sense of humor and patience when using these tools.

Next, let's discuss the power of non-verbal communication. Did you know that up to 93% of communication is non-verbal? This means that even if you don't speak the same language, you can still communicate effectively with your date. Use emoticons, GIFs, and stickers to express your emotions. These visual cues can help you convey your feelings more accurately, adding depth to your conversations.

Another strategy to overcome language barriers is to learn your date's language. Now, this doesn't mean that you need to become fluent overnight. However, learning a few basic phrases can go a long way in showing your interest and respect for your date's culture. Plus, it can be a fun and engaging activity that you both can participate in.

Finally, remember that communication is not just about speaking, it's also about listening. Active listening involves understanding the emotions and intentions behind the words. So, even if you don't understand every word your date says, try to understand their feelings. This will help you build a deeper connection.

In conclusion, language barriers are not a dead-end in your Facebook dating journey. They are merely detours that can lead you to exciting and unexplored paths. With the right mindset and strategies, you can turn these barriers into stepping stones that lead you towards a fulfilling relationship. So, don't let language barriers deter you. Instead, embrace them as opportunities to create unforgettable memories and deepen your bond with your date.

Dating with Children

Navigating the dating world as a single parent can seem daunting. However, with the right approach, you can strike the perfect balance between your love life and parenting responsibilities. Facebook Dating, a remarkable platform, can make this journey smoother for you.

Let's face it, being a single parent and trying to date can sometimes feel like juggling too many balls. It can be difficult to find time for yourself, and even harder to dedicate that time to finding a new partner. But, that's where Facebook Dating comes in. This platform allows you to connect with potential partners at your own pace and on your own time. You can browse through profiles during your lunch break or chat with someone interesting once the kids are in bed.

However, it's crucial to remember that honesty is the best policy. When setting up your Facebook Dating profile, be upfront about having children. This openness not only prevents misunderstandings down the line but also helps you attract the right kind of people—those who understand and respect your responsibilities as a parent.

Also, when using Facebook Dating, you can utilize its unique features to your advantage. For instance, the 'Secret Crush' option allows you to select up to nine of your Facebook friends or Instagram followers who you're interested in. If they join Facebook Dating and add you to their 'Secret Crush' list, it's a match! This feature can be especially beneficial for single parents, as it may help you find love among people you already know and trust.

Facebook Dating also prioritizes safety. Its 'Share Your Plans' feature allows you to share details of your date with a trusted friend. This added layer of security can be comforting for single parents who are understandably more cautious about their dating life.

But what about introducing your date to your children? This is a significant step that should be handled delicately. It's essential to wait until the relationship is serious and stable. Once you decide to take this step, Facebook Dating can help ease the process. You can share photos or videos of your children on your profile, letting your potential partner get to know them gradually. This can make the eventual face-to-face meeting less intimidating for all parties involved.

Moreover, remember that while dating as a single parent can be challenging, it's also an opportunity to model healthy relationships for your children. They will observe how you set boundaries, communicate, and show respect in your romantic relationships. Thus, not only are you seeking happiness for yourself, but you're also teaching your children valuable life lessons.

In conclusion, dating as a single parent doesn't have to be a daunting task. With Facebook Dating, you can meet potential partners in a safe and comfortable environment, all while managing your parenting responsibilities. So, take the plunge and give Facebook Dating a try. You never know, love could be just a click away!

Chapter 10: Safety Tips

Protecting Your Personal Information

In the realm of online dating, your personal information is your most valuable asset. It is the key to your identity, your security, and your peace of mind. You wouldn't hand over the keys to your house to a stranger, would you? Then why would you expose your most personal details on a platform like Facebook Dating without taking the necessary precautions? This chapter is dedicated to ensuring your safety while making the most of your online dating experience.

It is essential to remember that while Facebook Dating is a feature offered by the social media giant, it doesn't mean you should lower your guard. Your personal information should be as protected here as it is on any other platform. The first step is to understand what information Facebook Dating collects and how it uses it. This understanding will empower you to make informed decisions about what you choose to share.

While Facebook Dating makes use of your existing Facebook profile, it doesn't display your dating activity on your main profile. This separation of your dating and social profiles offers an added layer of privacy. However, it doesn't mean you should be complacent. Be mindful of the information you disclose in your dating profile. Avoid sharing sensitive details like your home address, workplace, or financial information.

Next, consider your interactions with potential matches. While it's natural to want to share details about your life to connect on a deeper level, it's essential to maintain a certain level of discretion. Until you've built a solid foundation of trust, it's wise to keep certain details to yourself. Remember, online predators often use the guise of romance to extract personal information.

Your photographs are also a part of your personal information. They can reveal more about you than you realize. For instance, a picture in front of your house can expose your residence location. Similarly, a photo of your car could reveal its make and model, which could be used to track you. Therefore, be careful with the photos you choose to upload.

In addition to being cautious about what you share, it's also important to use the privacy options provided by Facebook Dating. Make use of features like blocking and reporting for any suspicious activity. You can also restrict who can view your Dating profile to enhance your privacy.

Facebook Dating also offers a unique feature called Secret Crush. This allows you to select up to nine of your Facebook friends or Instagram followers who you're interested in. If they're also using Facebook Dating and add you as their Secret Crush, it's a match! While this feature can be exciting, it's also important to use it responsibly. Don't let the thrill of a potential match cloud your judgment when it comes to protecting your personal information.

In conclusion, while Facebook Dating can be a fun and effective way to meet potential partners, it's crucial to prioritize your safety. By being mindful of what you share, utilizing the privacy features, and maintaining a level of discretion, you can enjoy the journey of online dating without compromising your personal information. Remember, your safety and privacy are not a game of chance, but a matter of choice. Make the right one.

Avoiding Scams

As we delve deeper into the fascinating world of Facebook Dating, it's important to remember that not everyone in the virtual universe has noble intentions. Hence, the significance of avoiding scams cannot be overstated. This chapter will equip you with the necessary knowledge to keep you safe while you navigate your online dating journey, ensuring that you can confidently and securely explore the possibilities that Facebook Dating offers.

The first rule in avoiding scams is to always trust your instincts. If something feels off, it usually is. Scammers often prey on those who are willing to overlook red flags in their quest for love. Hence, always listen to your gut feelings. If a person's profile seems too good to be true, or if they're always making excuses to avoid meeting in person, it's best to proceed with caution.

Next, it's important to verify the identity of the person you're conversing with. Facebook Dating, like any other online platform, can be a breeding ground for catfishes – individuals who pretend to be someone they're not. They might use fake photos, create false backgrounds, or even steal someone else's identity. One way to verify someone's identity is by asking them to video chat. If they consistently refuse or make excuses, it could be a sign that they're not who they say they are.

Another common scam in online dating is the money scam. This usually involves the scammer trying to convince you to send them money, often for a seemingly good cause like a medical emergency or travel expenses to come and meet you. Remember, legitimate users of Facebook Dating will never ask you for money. If someone does, report them immediately and cease all communication.

It's also crucial to protect your personal information. Never share sensitive data like your home address, bank details, or social security number. Scammers can use this information for identity theft or other fraudulent activities. Even seemingly harmless information like your mother's maiden name or your pet's name can be used to answer security questions and gain access to your accounts. Be vigilant and always prioritize your safety.

Moreover, always report suspicious behavior. Facebook has stringent policies against scams and takes user reports seriously. If you encounter a profile that seems sketchy, or if someone is making you uncomfortable, don't hesitate to report them. This not only protects you but also helps keep the community safe for other users.

Finally, remember that online dating should be fun and enjoyable. Don't let the fear of scams deter you from exploring this exciting avenue. Instead, arm yourself with knowledge and stay vigilant. This will allow you to confidently navigate the world of Facebook Dating, knowing that you are well-equipped to protect yourself.

In conclusion, while the world of Facebook Dating offers exciting possibilities, it's important to remember that not everyone may have the best intentions. By trusting your instincts, verifying identities, protecting your personal information, and reporting suspicious behavior, you can enjoy your online dating journey while staying safe from potential scams. Remember, it's always better to be safe than sorry, and taking these precautions can save you from potential heartbreak and financial loss.

Meeting Safely in Person

Now, you've successfully navigated the exciting world of Facebook Dating, and you've connected with someone who piques your interest. It's time to take the leap and meet in person. However, amidst all the excitement and anticipation, it's crucial to remember the importance of prioritizing your safety. This is not to instill fear or paranoia, but to ensure that you can fully enjoy this new connection with peace of mind.

First and foremost, always meet in a public place. This is a golden rule of online dating safety. The positive buzz of people around creates a relaxed environment and lessens the chances of any untoward incidents. Choose a spot you're familiar with, like your favorite coffee shop or a popular local park. This familiarity will not only make you feel more comfortable but also gives you control over the setting.

Secondly, let someone close to you know about your plans. It can be a best friend, a sibling, or even a roommate. Share the details of your date - the time, the place, and the person you're meeting. This straightforward act can provide an extra layer of security. It's also a good idea to set up a safe call or text with this person during the date, just to check in.

Next, trust your instincts. You've been blessed with an intuitive sense for a reason. If something feels off, don't ignore it. It's better to end the date early or even cancel it altogether rather than risk your safety. Remember, you owe no explanations or apologies for prioritizing your well-being.

It's also advisable to manage your own transportation. Having your own ride allows you to leave whenever you want without relying on your date. If you don't drive, make sure you have a ride-hailing app installed on your phone. This way, you maintain control over your movements and can make a swift exit if needed.

Lastly, keep your personal information private. In the excitement of meeting someone new, it's easy to share more than necessary. Keep details like your home address, financial information, and other sensitive data to yourself until you're comfortable and have built a foundation of trust.

Meeting someone new from the Facebook Dating platform can be an exhilarating experience, and it should be. The thrill of the unknown, the butterflies in your stomach, the potential of a new romantic connection - they all add to the magic of dating. However, it's essential to balance this excitement with a healthy dose of caution.

Remember, your safety is paramount. By following these guidelines, you're not only protecting yourself, but you're also setting the stage for a more relaxed and enjoyable dating experience. These measures don't make you paranoid; they make you prepared. So, go ahead, step out confidently into this exciting new chapter of your dating life. After all, you're not just opening the doors to potential love but also to a world of exciting possibilities.

Trust Your Instincts

As you navigate the complex world of Facebook dating, your instincts will be your most reliable compass. This is not mere conjecture; it's a proven fact that our gut feelings often guide us toward the best decisions. So, when it comes to your Facebook dating journey, don't ignore those hunches. They might just lead you to the love of your life.

Now, you might be wondering, "How exactly do I trust my instincts in dating?" Well, it's simple. It's about listening to that little voice in your head that tells you when something feels right...or when it doesn't. It's about recognizing the flutter in your stomach, the quickening of your pulse, or the unease creeping at the back of your mind. These are all signs that your instincts are trying to communicate with you.

For instance, you're scrolling through Facebook, and you come across a profile that catches your eye. You're drawn to their photos, their interests, and their witty status updates. But then, you get a nagging feeling that something isn't quite right. Maybe it's a comment they made, or a photo that doesn't quite match up with what they've told you. That's your instincts kicking in, telling you to proceed with caution. Listen to them.

On the other hand, you may find a profile that doesn't immediately stand out to you. They don't have the flashiest photos or the most followers, but as you interact with them, you feel a sense of ease and comfort. You find yourself smiling at their messages and looking forward to their replies. That's your instincts telling you that this person might be worth getting to know better.

However, trusting your instincts doesn't mean you should make snap judgments. It's not about dismissing someone because of a single comment or photo. It's about paying attention to how you feel as you interact with them over time. It's about noticing patterns and considering whether they align with what you're looking for in a partner.

Also, remember that your instincts are deeply personal. What feels right for you might not feel right for someone else, and vice versa. So, don't let others sway your decisions. Trusting your instincts means standing by your feelings, even when others might not understand.

It's also worth noting that trusting your instincts is not an excuse for being judgmental or prejudiced. It's not about rejecting someone because they don't fit your ideal image of a partner. It's about being honest with yourself about how you feel, and making decisions that honor those feelings.

In the world of Facebook dating, there will be countless profiles to scroll through, messages to exchange, and people to meet. It can be overwhelming. But remember, you have a built-in guide: your instincts. Trust them. Listen to them. They might just lead you to the love of your life.

So, as you continue your Facebook dating journey, remember to trust your instincts. They are your most reliable compass, guiding you towards the relationships that will enrich your life and bring you joy. Trusting your instincts is not just a dating strategy; it's a way of honoring your feelings and making decisions that are truly right for you.

Reporting Misconduct

The essence of any relationship, be it online or offline, is trust and respect. When these are violated, it creates a harmful environment, not just for the individuals involved but also for the community as a whole. In the world of Facebook dating, it's no different. Misconduct should never be tolerated. But, how can we ensure that? How can we contribute to a safer and more respectful digital dating environment? It's simple. By reporting misconduct.

If you encounter any unpleasant or harmful behavior while using Facebook Dating, it's not just your right, but also your duty to report it. This is not just about standing up for yourself, but also about protecting others who might fall victim to the same misconduct. Remember, your voice matters. Your actions can make a difference.

When it comes to reporting misconduct, there are a few key points you need to remember. Firstly, it's crucial to provide as much detail as possible. This will help the Facebook team to take appropriate action. Secondly, remember that you can report any user or conversation that makes you uncomfortable. It's not about being overly sensitive; it's about ensuring a respectful and safe environment for everyone.

The act of reporting is not just about punishment for the wrongdoer, but also about education. It's about teaching people what is acceptable behavior and what is not. It's about setting standards for our online interactions, just as we do in our offline world. We are all part of this digital community, and we all have a role to play in shaping it.

But what happens after you report misconduct? Rest assured, Facebook takes these matters very seriously. Your report will be reviewed by a team of specialists who are trained to handle such situations. They will investigate the matter thoroughly and take appropriate action. Your identity will be kept confidential, so you don't have to worry about any backlash.

It's important to remember that reporting misconduct is not about creating a culture of fear or mistrust. It's about creating a culture of respect and dignity. It's about standing up against inappropriate behavior and ensuring that

Facebook Dating remains a safe and positive space for everyone.

In conclusion, reporting misconduct on Facebook Dating is not just a tool for self-protection, but a service to the entire community. It is a way to enforce the standards of respect and safety that we all deserve. It sends a clear message that inappropriate behavior will not be tolerated. So, don't hesitate. If you encounter any misconduct, report it. Stand up for yourself and for your fellow Facebook daters. You have the power to make a difference. You have the power to shape the world of Facebook Dating. Use it wisely.

Chapter 11: Success Stories

Long Distance Love

In this age of digital connectivity, love has extended its reach beyond geographical boundaries. Yes, we're talking about long-distance relationships, a phenomenon that has been made possible and more prevalent by social media platforms such as Facebook. Facebook, with its expansive network of people from all corners of the globe, has become a modern-day Cupid, connecting hearts across continents and oceans.

You might be skeptical about finding love on Facebook, especially if it comes with the challenges of distance. But let's debunk some myths. The distance, rather than being a hindrance, can be a catalyst for stronger bonds and deeper connections. It's not the physical distance that matters, but the emotional closeness that two people share. And Facebook, with its various communication features, provides ample opportunities to nurture this emotional closeness.

With Facebook, you can communicate with your love interest in real time, regardless of the time zone differences. You can share your daily experiences, feelings, and thoughts through posts, photos, and videos. The Messenger feature allows for intimate one-on-one conversations, while the comment section gives room for public displays of affection.

Facebook Dating is another feature that makes it easier to find love from afar. It's a dedicated space within the Facebook app, designed to facilitate meaningful relationships. You can set preferences based on your interests, and Facebook will suggest potential matches. This feature is particularly useful if you're open to exploring love beyond your locality.

However, diving into the world of long-distance love via Facebook requires a certain level of tact and understanding. Privacy is paramount. You should respect your partner's online space just as you would respect their physical space. It's also important to maintain a balance between online and offline communication. While Facebook is a great tool for staying connected, nothing replaces the value of face-to-face communication.

Trust is another crucial element in a long-distance relationship. It's easy to become insecure when your partner is miles away, but remember that trust is the foundation of any relationship. Facebook can be a tool to build trust, but it can also be a tool to break it. Be transparent with your online activities, and avoid any behavior that could breed suspicion or doubt.

Lastly, remember that every relationship is unique. What works for one couple might not work for another. Thus, it's important to find your own rhythm and dynamics. Facebook is just a tool that can help you maintain your relationship. The real work lies in the commitment, understanding, and love that both partners put into the relationship.

In conclusion, Facebook has indeed revolutionized the way we perceive and pursue love. It has broken down geographical barriers and opened up a world of possibilities for long-distance love. But like any tool, it should be used wisely and responsibly. With the right approach, Facebook can indeed be the bridge that connects two hearts, regardless of the distance between them.

Finding Love After 50

You might be thinking that the digital age of dating is only for the young and tech-savvy. But let me assure you, it's never too late to find love, and age is just a number. Yes, even if you're over 50, the world of online dating is as accessible to you as it is to anyone else. Facebook, a platform you are likely already familiar with, offers a dating feature that is simple and easy to use. It's time to debunk the myth that online dating is a young person's game.

Facebook Dating is not just for millennials. It's a platform designed for everyone, irrespective of age. It's an opportunity for you to connect with like-minded individuals, find companionship, and yes, even love. The idea of starting over can be daunting, but Facebook Dating makes it easier. It offers a safe, comfortable, and convenient platform where you can meet potential partners.

You might be questioning, "Why would I turn to Facebook for dating?" The answer is simple: familiarity and convenience. You're probably already using Facebook to connect with friends and family, share photos, and catch up on news. Why not use it to find love as well? Facebook Dating is an extension of the Facebook you already know and use daily.

With Facebook Dating, you're not starting from scratch. The platform uses the information you've already provided to Facebook to help you meet people with similar interests, in your preferred age range. You can even see if you have mutual friends with potential matches, providing an extra layer of security and comfort.

You might be concerned about privacy, and rightly so. But with Facebook Dating, your dating profile is separate from your regular Facebook profile, and your dating activity won't be shared with anyone on your friend's list. You have complete control over who sees your dating profile and who doesn't.

One of the most compelling reasons to give Facebook Dating a try is its unique feature called "Secret Crush." This feature allows you to select up to nine of your Facebook friends or Instagram followers who you're interested in. If they're also using Facebook Dating and they add you to their Secret Crush list, it's a match! This feature is an excellent way to explore potential relationships within your existing circles, without the risk of embarrassment or rejection.

Finding love is not about age; it's about finding someone who complements you and understands you. It's about finding someone who will walk with you during the golden years of your life. Facebook Dating provides you with the tools you need to find that person.

Don't let your age deter you from exploring this new world of dating. Embrace the digital age and use it to your advantage. Remember, age is just a number, and it's never too late to find love. Facebook is not just a social networking site anymore; it's a platform that can help you find love, no matter how old you are.

In conclusion, Facebook Dating is not just for the young; it's for the young at heart. It's for those who believe in love, irrespective of age. So, why not give it a try? After all, love could be just a click away.

Second Chance at Love

If you've been unlucky in love before, don't be disheartened. The world of Facebook Dating presents you with a golden opportunity to find love again. The past is gone, and it's time to embrace the present. This is your second chance at love, and it's time to seize it.

Facebook Dating is not just another dating platform. It's an innovative, convenient, and comprehensive tool that allows you to meet people who share your interests, values, and aspirations. The algorithms of Facebook Dating are designed to match you with potential partners who are most likely to be compatible with you. This significantly increases your chances of finding someone who could be your perfect match.

Perhaps you have been hurt in the past, and the idea of opening your heart again seems daunting. But remember, everyone deserves love and happiness, and that includes you. The beauty of Facebook Dating is that it allows you to take things at your own pace. You can take your time to get to know someone before deciding whether to meet them in person. This gives you the control and the confidence to step back into the dating scene.

Moreover, Facebook Dating has a unique 'Second Look' feature. This allows you to revisit potential matches you may have initially skipped over. Sometimes, initial impressions can be deceiving, and this feature gives you a chance to reconsider, just in case you missed your perfect match. This is a literal embodiment of a second chance at love.

The platform also allows you to express your true self through your profile. You can share your interests, passions, and what you're looking for in a partner. This level of transparency helps potential matches get a sense of who you are, increasing the likelihood of meaningful connections.

You don't have to worry about your privacy either. Facebook Dating takes your security seriously. Your dating activity will not be shared with your Facebook friends, and you have the power to decide who can see your dating profile.

Don't let fear or past experiences hold you back. It's time to give love a second chance. The person you've been waiting for could be just a click away. Remember, the universe works in mysterious ways, and love often finds us when we least expect it.

In conclusion, Facebook Dating offers a unique and innovative platform for you to find love again. Its advanced features, user-friendly interface, and commitment to privacy make it an ideal choice for those looking for a second chance at love. The past may have been filled with heartache and disappointment, but the future holds infinite possibilities. All you need to do is take the first step, open your heart, and let love in once again. So why wait? Give Facebook Dating a try today, and you might just find that second chance at love you've been longing for.

Love at First Swipe

Imagine, if you will, a world where your next love interest is just a swipe away. A world where you don't have to rely on fate or chance encounters, but on the power of social media. This is the world of Facebook Dating, where love can happen at first swipe.

Facebook Dating is not just another dating app. It's a revolutionary platform that uses advanced algorithms to match you with potential partners based on shared interests, mutual friends, and even events you both plan to attend. But how do you navigate this digital landscape of love? The key is understanding how to use the platform to your advantage.

Firstly, it's important to remember that Facebook Dating is more than just a game of swipes. It's about making meaningful connections. To do this, you need to carefully curate your profile. Your profile is your first impression, so make it count. Use clear, high-quality photos that showcase your personality and interests. Keep your bio interesting and engaging. Remember, your potential match will be deciding whether to swipe right based on this information.

Next, be proactive. Don't just wait for matches to come to you. Use the search function to find people who share your interests and values. Send them a thoughtful message to show that you're genuinely interested in getting to know them. This can set you apart from the crowd and increase your chances of finding a meaningful connection.

But what about the actual swiping? It's easy to get caught up in the thrill of the game, but remember that each swipe is a potential match. Don't just swipe right on anyone. Be selective. Take the time to read each profile and consider whether you could see a future with this person. This can save you time and heartache in the long run.

Facebook Dating also offers unique features that can help you stand out. The Secret Crush feature allows you to express interest in a friend without them knowing, unless they feel the same way. The Event and Group features allow you to connect with people who are attending the same events or are part of the same groups. These features can give you a head start in finding someone with similar interests.

Finally, remember to be patient. Love at first swipe is possible, but it may not happen immediately. It may take time to find the right person. Don't get discouraged if you don't find a match right away. Keep refining your profile, keep searching, and keep swiping. Your perfect match could be just a swipe away.

Facebook Dating is an exciting new frontier in the world of online dating. It combines the familiarity of Facebook with the thrill of finding love. With the right approach, you can navigate this platform with ease and find your love at first swipe. So, what are you waiting for? Start swiping and start loving today!

From Friends to Lovers

If you've made it this far into the book, then you're well on your way to mastering the art of Facebook dating. Now, let's address the most exciting part of the journey - transitioning from friends to lovers. This can be a delicate process, but with the right approach, you can turn your Facebook friend into your romantic partner.

The first step is understanding the difference between friendship and romantic interest. A friend is someone you share common interests with, enjoy spending time with, and can trust. A lover, on the other hand, is someone you are physically attracted to, someone who you desire to share an emotional bond with, and someone you can see a future with. Recognizing this distinction is crucial for the transition.

Now that you understand the difference, it's time to subtly show your romantic interest. Start by liking and reacting to their posts more frequently and more enthusiastically. This will signal your increased interest in them without coming off as too eager or desperate.

Next, engage them in deeper, more personal conversations. Move beyond the typical 'how was your day' or 'what are you up to' and delve into their dreams, passions, and fears. This will not only show that you're genuinely interested in them, but also that you're someone they can open up to and trust, both of which are essential in a romantic relationship.

Once you've set the stage, it's time to take the bold step. Invite them out for a casual, non-threatening outing. This could be anything from a coffee date to a walk in the park. The key here is to create an environment where you can both relax and enjoy each other's company outside of the digital world.

During this outing, pay close attention to their body language and reactions. If they seem comfortable and engaged, this is a good sign that they might also be interested in taking the relationship to the next level. On the other hand, if they seem distant or uninterested, it might be best to back off and remain friends.

If all goes well, it's time to express your feelings. Be honest and straightforward, but also gentle and understanding. Let them know that you value your friendship, but also that you've developed deeper feelings for them.

Remember, being turned down is a possibility. If this happens, it's important to respect their decision and continue to value your friendship. After all, not every friend is meant to become a lover.

However, if they reciprocate your feelings, congratulations! You've successfully navigated the tricky transition from friends to lovers.

In conclusion, moving from friends to lovers on Facebook is a delicate process that requires a deep understanding of the difference between friendship and love, subtle signals of interest, deeper conversations, a casual outing, and finally, expressing your feelings. If done correctly, you can turn your Facebook friend into your romantic partner.

Remember, the most important thing is to stay true to yourself and respect the other person's feelings and decisions. Happy dating!

Chapter 12: Tips for LGBTQ+ Dating

Creating an Inclusive Profile

In the realm of online dating, your profile serves as your first impression, your virtual handshake, your introduction to potential love interests. In the vast digital sea of Facebook Dating, it is your beacon, calling out to like-minded souls. It's your chance to show your most authentic self, capturing both your personality and your intentions. So, how do you craft a profile that is not just attractive, but also inclusive?

Firstly, remember that inclusivity begins with respect. You are stepping into a space that is as diverse as it is vast. The users you'll encounter come from various walks of life, each with their own unique stories, experiences, and perspectives. Your profile should reflect an open-mindedness towards this diversity. This is not just about being politically correct; it's about fostering an environment of mutual respect and understanding.

Start with your profile picture. This is the first thing people see, and it can set the tone for the rest of your profile. Choose a photo that is both flattering and honest. It should represent who you are and what you look like now, not five years or twenty pounds ago. Avoid group photos where it's hard to tell who you are or pictures with exes. This isn't just about being clear; it's about being respectful of others' time and efforts.

Next, take the time to fill out your profile completely. The more information you provide, the easier it is for potential matches to see if you share common interests or life goals. Be honest about who you are and what you're looking for. If you're not interested in a long-term relationship, say so. If you're looking for something serious, make that clear. Honesty is not just attractive; it's inclusive. It respects others' feelings and intentions, and it helps avoid misunderstandings down the line.

When filling out your profile, be mindful of your language. Avoid offensive or divisive language. This includes slurs, offensive jokes, or anything that could be seen as disrespectful or prejudiced. Remember, you're not just representing yourself; you're also representing the kind of environment you want to create.

When talking about your interests or hobbies, try to be as broad as possible. You might be surprised at how many people share your love for obscure indie bands or your passion for bird watching. But remember, it's not just about attracting people who share your interests; it's about attracting people who respect and appreciate your interests.

When it comes to your 'About Me' section, strive for balance. Share enough about yourself to spark interest, but leave some things to the imagination. This creates a sense of mystery and gives potential matches something to ask about.

Finally, always be open to feedback. If someone points out something problematic in your profile, listen and learn. This doesn't mean you have to change who you are; it just means you have to be willing to grow and adapt.

Remember, creating an inclusive profile isn't just about attracting as many people as possible. It's about attracting the right people, those who will respect and appreciate you for who you are. It's about creating a space where everyone feels welcome and respected. And ultimately, it's about paving the way for meaningful connections and relationships.

Navigating the Dating Scene

As we venture into the world of Facebook Dating, it's essential to understand the landscape and how to successfully navigate it. Let's liken the dating scene to a vast ocean, teeming with diverse sea life, where you're the captain of your boat, seeking the right catch. You wouldn't set sail without a map or compass, would you? Similarly, diving into Facebook dating without a plan can lead to aimless wandering, frustration, and even potential heartbreak.

Firstly, you must know what you're looking for. Are you seeking a casual fling, a serious relationship, or just expanding your social circle? Being clear about your intentions will help you filter potential matches and conversations, saving you time and effort. Remember, the beauty of Facebook Dating is its vast user base, so there's something for everybody.

Secondly, be confident and authentic. In the world of online dating, people appreciate genuineness. Let your profile reflect your true self. Your pictures, interests, and bio should paint an accurate picture of who you are. Avoid the temptation to embellish or create a persona that isn't you. Remember, the goal is to attract people who will appreciate and connect with the real you.

Interacting with potential matches is another crucial aspect of navigating Facebook Dating. When initiating conversations, be respectful, show genuine interest, and keep the conversation light and engaging. Avoid controversial topics or anything that might create an uncomfortable atmosphere. Remember, the goal is to establish a connection and get to know each other better.

Remember to be patient. Love is not a race; it's a journey. You might not find your perfect match immediately, but don't get disheartened. Keep interacting, stay positive, and keep your options open.

Safety should be your top priority. While Facebook Dating has various safety features, it's crucial to be vigilant. Avoid sharing personal information such as your home address, bank details, or anything that could be misused. If something feels off about a person or conversation, trust your instincts and disengage.

Lastly, enjoy the process. Dating should be fun, not a chore. Embrace the opportunity to meet new people, learn about different cultures and lifestyles, and possibly find love. Remember, every interaction, whether successful or not, is a learning experience that brings you one step closer to finding your perfect match.

In conclusion, navigating the Facebook Dating scene is about understanding what you want, being genuine, interacting respectfully, being patient, prioritizing safety, and enjoying the process. It's about sailing through the vast ocean, appreciating the beauty of the journey, and eventually finding your treasure. Don't rush the process; instead, embrace the adventure that comes with it.

Remember, Facebook Dating is just a tool in your dating arsenal. It's a platform that provides opportunities, but it's up to you to seize them. So, captain, are you ready to set sail? The ocean of Facebook Dating awaits you, teeming with potential matches and exciting experiences. Unfurl your sails, hold on to your compass, and embark on this thrilling journey.

Understanding Gender Identities

In today's digital era, understanding gender identities is a critical component of the dating landscape, especially when navigating social platforms like Facebook. In the context of

Facebook dating, understanding and respecting a person's gender identity can significantly impact your online dating success. It's not just about being politically correct; it's about being a compassionate, informed, and considerate individual.

Facebook, like many other social media platforms, has evolved to recognize a spectrum of gender identities. It's no longer a binary world of 'male' and 'female.' In fact, Facebook currently offers more than 50 options for users to identify their gender, including identities such as non-binary, genderqueer, and two-spirit, to name a few. This progressive move is a reflection of our society's growing understanding of gender as a complex construct that goes beyond biological sex.

So, how does this tie into Facebook dating? Well, it's simple. When you understand and respect someone's gender identity, you show them that you see them for who they truly are. This acceptance can create a strong foundation for a potential relationship. It's about recognizing that everyone has the right to express their identity and live authentically. After all, isn't that what we're all seeking in a relationship – to be loved and accepted for who we are?

As you navigate Facebook dating, consider how you can show respect for all gender identities. This might involve educating yourself about different gender identities, using the correct pronouns, or showing support for your potential match's gender identity. It can also mean standing up against transphobia and other forms of discrimination that people of diverse gender identities face.

Understanding gender identities is not just about paying lip service to inclusivity. It's about creating a space where everyone feels seen, validated, and respected. It's about fostering a culture of empathy and understanding on a platform that connects millions of people worldwide.

In the realm of Facebook dating, this understanding can be a game-changer. It can help you connect on a deeper level with potential matches, fostering meaningful conversations and genuine connections. It can make your profile stand out as one that is inclusive and respectful, attracting like-minded individuals who value these qualities.

In the end, understanding gender identities can make you a better dater and a better person. It can broaden your perspective, enrich your relationships, and deepen your understanding of the diverse world we live in. It's not just a trend or a buzzword; it's a fundamental aspect of human identity that deserves recognition and respect.

So, as you explore the world of Facebook dating, remember to keep an open mind. Embrace the diversity of gender identities, and let this understanding guide your interactions. After all, love knows no gender. It's about the connection between two people, regardless of how they identify. In recognizing and respecting this, you'll be one step closer to finding your perfect match on Facebook.

Dealing with Discrimination

In the realm of online dating, an unfortunate reality that we must confront is the presence of discrimination. It is a pervasive issue that often goes unaddressed, silently shaping the experiences of countless individuals. Let's be clear: discrimination, in any form, is unacceptable. When it comes to Facebook dating, it's crucial to understand how to effectively handle such situations and foster a more inclusive and respectful community.

Discrimination can take on many forms, from ageism and sexism to racism and homophobia. It's an ugly side of human nature, often rooted in ignorance, fear, or a misguided sense of superiority. But remember, it is not your responsibility to educate or change the minds of those who discriminate against you. Your responsibility is to protect your mental and emotional well-being, and to ensure your online dating experience is as positive and fruitful as possible.

Firstly, always report discriminatory behavior. Facebook has implemented robust reporting mechanisms to ensure a safe and respectful environment for its users. By reporting, you not only protect yourself but also help Facebook in identifying and taking action against those who violate their community guidelines. This is a significant step towards creating a more inclusive and respectful online dating community.

Secondly, do not engage in arguments or heated exchanges with those who discriminate against you. It may be tempting to defend yourself or attempt to enlighten the other person, but more often than not, you'll only fuel the fire and give them more reason to continue their inappropriate behavior. Instead, block them. This simple action will prevent further communication, safeguarding your peace of mind.

Remember, it's essential to foster a positive self-image and not let the discriminatory views of others affect your self-esteem. You are more than the color of your skin, your age, your gender, or who you choose to love. You are a unique individual, deserving of respect and love. Don't let anyone's narrow-minded views make you feel less than that.

Moreover, be an ally. If you witness discriminatory behavior towards others, don't be a bystander. Report it. Stand up for others when they are unable to do so for themselves. By doing this, we can collectively create a more respectful and inclusive environment for everyone.

Finally, it's important to remember that not all experiences on Facebook dating will be negative. There are countless success stories of people finding love and forming meaningful connections. Don't let the actions of a few discourage you from exploring the potential of online dating.

In conclusion, dealing with discrimination can be an unpleasant experience, but it's not an insurmountable obstacle. By taking the right steps, we can effectively handle such situations and contribute to a more inclusive and respectful online dating community. We should never let discrimination deter us from our quest for love and companionship. After all, everyone deserves to find their perfect match, free from prejudice and bias.

Safe Dating Tips

When it comes to online dating, safety should be your top priority. This is particularly true for Facebook dating, where the virtual world offers a myriad of opportunities to connect, but also poses significant risks. So, as you venture into the exciting world of Facebook dating, here are some tips to ensure your safety.

Firstly, it's crucial to protect your personal information. While Facebook dating offers an easy way to meet new people, it's essential to remember that not everyone on the platform may have good intentions. Be cautious about the information you share and avoid disclosing sensitive details such as your home address, workplace, or financial information.

Secondly, take your time. Just because you've matched with someone on Facebook doesn't mean you should rush into meeting them in person. Spend time getting to know them online first. Watch for red flags, such as inconsistent stories or aggressive behavior. If something doesn't feel right, trust your instincts.

Thirdly, when you decide to meet in person, choose a public place. Meeting in a crowded area will not only make you feel more comfortable but also safer. It's also a good idea to let a friend or family member know where you're going and who you're meeting.

Fourthly, be wary of catfishing. It's a deceptive technique where someone creates a fake profile to trick others into a relationship. If your match's photos look too good to be true, they refuse to video call, or their life story seems too perfect, they might be a catfish. Always do a quick search of their photos or details to verify their genuineness.

Fifthly, remember that no one should pressure you into anything. Whether it's sharing personal information, meeting in person, or engaging in sexual activities, you should always feel comfortable with your decisions. If someone is pressuring you, it's a clear sign that they don't respect your boundaries, and it's best to cut ties with them.

Lastly, don't be afraid to report any suspicious behavior. Facebook has a dedicated team to handle such issues, and it's vital to report any incidents that make you uncomfortable. This will not only protect you but also help safeguard others on the platform.

In conclusion, while Facebook dating can be an exciting way to meet new people, it's crucial to prioritize your safety. By safeguarding your personal information, taking your time, choosing safe meeting places, being aware of catfishing, respecting your boundaries, and reporting suspicious behavior, you can enjoy the benefits of Facebook dating while mitigating the risks.

Remember, the true essence of dating is to have fun and perhaps find a meaningful connection. So, don't let the fear of risks rob you of the joy that Facebook dating can bring. Instead, equip yourself with these safety tips, and step into the world of Facebook dating with confidence. After all, when you are safe and secure, you are in the best position to open your heart and truly connect with others.

In the end, it's about striking a balance between keeping your guard up and letting your guard down. Keep these tips in mind, and you'll not only be safe but also have the best chance of finding that special someone on Facebook.

Chapter 13: Tips for Disabled Dating

Creating a Positive Profile

Imagine this: you're scrolling through your Facebook feed, and you come across a profile that immediately captures your attention. The profile picture is of a person beaming with genuine happiness, their bio is engaging and intriguing, and their posts are a perfect mix of fun, thought-provoking, and personal. You feel an immediate connection, and you can't help but click the 'like' button. Now, wouldn't you want your dating profile to have that same effect on others?

Creating a positive profile is the first and most crucial step in your Facebook dating journey. It's your golden opportunity to make a compelling first impression, to showcase who you are, and to attract the kind of people you'd love to connect with.

Firstly, let's talk about your profile picture. It's the first thing people see, and it plays a significant role in whether someone will be interested in learning more about you. A picture can speak a thousand words, so make sure yours is saying all the right ones. Opt for a picture where you're smiling genuinely, dressed appropriately, and in a setting that reflects your personality. Avoid overly edited or filtered photos; authenticity is key in making a real connection.

Next, your bio. This is your chance to share a little about yourself. Keep it light, positive, and a bit mysterious. You want to pique people's interest and leave them wanting to know more. Share your passions, hobbies, or a quirky fact about yourself. Remember, your bio is not a resume; you don't need to list all your achievements or qualifications. It's more about showcasing your personality and what makes you unique.

Now, onto your posts. They are a reflection of your life and interests. Post content that aligns with who you are and what you love. Do you enjoy hiking? Share a picture from your latest adventure. Are you a foodie? Post about the delicious meal you've just cooked. Are you passionate about a cause? Share articles or posts related to it. Your posts should tell a story about you and your life.

However, while sharing, remember to maintain a balance. Don't overshare or make your profile a constant stream of selfies. Also, remember to be positive. No one is attracted to negativity. We all have our bad days, but your Facebook dating profile is not the place to vent.

Engage with others positively, too. Like and comment on posts that resonate with you. Show appreciation and respect in your interactions. This not only makes you more attractive but also helps you connect with like-minded people.

Lastly, privacy is paramount. Be cautious about the personal information you share. It's always better to err on the side of caution when it comes to your safety and privacy.

Creating a positive profile is not about pretending to be someone you're not. It's about presenting the best, most authentic version of yourself. It's about painting a picture of who you are and what you bring to the table. It's about using your profile as a tool to attract and connect with people who will appreciate and cherish you for who you are.

Remember, in the world of Facebook dating, your profile is your ambassador. Make it a good one. A positive, authentic, and engaging profile can be your ticket to finding meaningful connections and possibly, love. So go ahead, put your best foot forward, and create a profile that truly represents you.

Dating with a Disability

Navigating the dating world can be tricky for anyone, but it can be especially challenging for those with disabilities. However, this should not deter you from seeking love and companionship. Remember, everyone has the right to experience the joy of connection, and Facebook Dating provides an excellent platform to do so.

Facebook Dating, as an inclusive space, does not discriminate against anyone, including those with disabilities. It is designed to foster connections between all kinds of people, and it's high time we utilized it to its full potential and broke the stigmas surrounding disabled dating.

One of the primary benefits of Facebook Dating for individuals with disabilities is the ability to be upfront about your condition. This platform allows you to express yourself authentically, giving potential partners a clear understanding of who you are from the beginning. The key is to approach your disability with confidence, treating it as a part of your identity, not as a burden.

Moreover, Facebook Dating allows you to connect with people based on shared interests and values, rather than mere physical appearance. This ensures a deeper and more meaningful connection which is not solely reliant on physical abilities or appearances.

Facebook Dating also provides a safer environment for people with disabilities to begin their dating journey. You can take your time to get to know someone before meeting them in person, allowing you to build trust and establish a connection at your own pace. This eliminates the pressure of first-date nerves and allows you to focus on the person, not the disability.

However, it's crucial to remember that not everyone on Facebook Dating may understand your situation. It's essential to remain patient and open-minded, ready to educate others about your disability if necessary. Don't be disheartened by ignorance or lack of understanding; instead, see it as an opportunity to enlighten others and potentially form a deep, meaningful relationship.

Additionally, Facebook Dating allows you to connect with other individuals who also have disabilities. This opens up a world of understanding and common ground, where you can share experiences, advice, and support. It can be incredibly empowering to connect with someone who understands your unique challenges and can provide a sense of camaraderie and kinship.

In conclusion, having a disability should never stand in the way of your quest for love. Facebook Dating provides a platform where you can be open, honest, and confident about your disability, connecting with people who appreciate you for who you are. It's about time we embraced the power of technology to break down barriers, challenge stereotypes, and create a more inclusive and accepting dating world for all.

Remember, your disability does not define you. You are a person worthy of love and connection, just like anyone else. So, take a deep breath, sign up for Facebook Dating, and start connecting. You never know, your perfect match could be just a click away.

Navigating Accessibility

Facebook Dating is a platform that offers a unique opportunity to connect with people who share similar interests. However, to unlock its full potential, it is crucial to understand how to navigate its accessibility features effectively.

Facebook Dating is designed to be user-friendly, making it easy for anyone, regardless of their technical expertise, to navigate. But, like any other tool, it is only as effective as your understanding of its features. So, let's demystify this journey and set you on the path to successful online dating.

Firstly, Facebook Dating is located right within the Facebook app, making it easily accessible to all Facebook users. You don't need to download a separate app or create a new account; instead, you can access it directly from your existing Facebook account. This seamless integration allows for a smooth transition and a comfortable user experience.

Now, you may wonder, "What about my privacy?" Well, Facebook Dating emphasizes user privacy and safety. Your dating profile is separate from your Facebook profile, and your Facebook friends won't be suggested as potential matches. This feature ensures an environment where you can explore new connections without worrying about privacy breaches.

To enhance your accessibility experience, Facebook Dating also offers a unique 'Secret Crush' feature. This feature allows you to select up to nine of your Facebook friends or Instagram followers who you're interested in. If they are also using Facebook Dating and add you to their 'Secret Crush' list, a match is made! It's a perfect blend of familiarity and surprise, making your dating journey exciting and comfortable.

Facebook Dating also offers a second chance with the 'Second Look' feature. It allows you to revisit suggested matches that you may have previously dismissed. This feature not only increases your chances of finding a suitable match but also provides a sense of control over your dating journey.

Moreover, Facebook Dating's preference settings offer a broad range of options, allowing you to customize your experience to suit your preferences. You can filter potential matches based on various factors like location, age, and interests. This feature allows you to narrow down your choices, making your search more efficient and less time-consuming.

However, the most significant feature that makes Facebook Dating stand out is its emphasis on shared interests. It suggests potential matches based on your shared interests, groups, and events. This feature ensures that you connect with like-minded individuals, making your dating experience more meaningful and less superficial.

In conclusion, Facebook Dating provides an accessible platform for online dating. Its user-friendly features ensure a smooth and comfortable user experience while prioritizing your privacy and safety. The 'Secret Crush' and 'Second Look' features add an element of excitement and control to your dating journey, while the preference settings and shared interest-based suggestions ensure efficient and meaningful connections.

So, are you ready to unlock the full potential of Facebook Dating? Remember, the key lies in understanding and navigating its accessibility features effectively. Now, go ahead and explore the world of Facebook Dating, and you might just find your perfect match!

Dealing with Prejudices

The world of Facebook dating can be both exciting and intimidating. It's a new realm of possibilities, a place where love might be just a click away. However, it is also a world that is often colored by prejudices, misconceptions, and biases. It's time to address these prejudices and clear the path towards successful Facebook dating.

Many people harbor the notion that online dating, including Facebook dating, is only for the desperate or the socially awkward. This couldn't be further from the truth. A plethora of individuals from all walks of life, with diverse interests, professions, and personalities, are now turning to online platforms to find love. Facebook dating is not just for the desperate; it's for everyone who is looking to expand their romantic horizons.

Another common prejudice is the belief that Facebook dating isn't safe. While it's true that online platforms have their fair share of risks, Facebook has implemented several safety measures to protect its users. From the ability to report and block users to options for sharing your live location with a friend during a date, Facebook dating prioritizes your safety. You have the tools to protect yourself, it's just a matter of using them wisely.

A third prejudice that often surfaces is the notion that relationships initiated through Facebook dating are not as serious or committed as those started offline. This is a myth. The medium through which a relationship begins doesn't determine its depth, commitment, or longevity. What matters are the people involved, their feelings, and their intentions. Many individuals have found meaningful, long-term relationships through Facebook dating, proving that this platform can indeed lead to true love.

Then, there's the misconception that Facebook dating is all about casual hook-ups and flings. While it's true that some people use it for this purpose, many others are genuinely seeking meaningful connections and relationships. Just like in the real world, the intentions of people on Facebook dating vary. It's up to you to communicate your expectations and find someone who aligns with them.

Let's also address the belief that Facebook dating lacks the excitement and romance of traditional dating. This is subjective and depends on how you use the platform. You can create excitement by engaging in interesting conversations, sharing pictures or videos, or even planning virtual dates. As for romance, it's not confined to physical spaces. Genuine compliments, deep conversations, shared interests – these can all create a romantic atmosphere, even in the digital world.

In conclusion, prejudices against Facebook dating are often based on misconceptions and stereotypes. They do not reflect the reality of this dynamic and diverse platform. Like any other form of dating, Facebook dating has its pros and cons. It's not perfect, but it's certainly not the desperate, unsafe, unromantic world that some people imagine it to be. So, let's discard these prejudices and approach Facebook dating with an open mind. After all, love can be found in the most unexpected places, and for many, that place could be Facebook.

Safe Dating Tips

As you navigate through the exciting world of Facebook dating, it is of utmost importance to prioritize your safety. We all dream of the perfect love story, but it's crucial to remember that not everyone has good intentions. Thus, protecting yourself should be your top priority.

Firstly, it's vital to recognize the importance of keeping your personal information private. While it's natural to want to share aspects of your life with potential matches, be cautious about revealing too much too soon. Keep your address, workplace, and financial information confidential until you've built trust with the person. Remember, your safety is more important than impressing a stranger with personal details.

Secondly, make sure to verify your match's identity. In the digital age, it's shockingly easy for individuals to pretend to be someone they're not. If your match's profile seems suspicious or too good to be true, it probably is. Use video calls to confirm their identity before you meet in person. This can save you from potential heartache and danger.

Thirdly, always meet in public places for your first few dates. This is not only a safety precaution but also a good practice for easing the initial awkwardness. Choose a location where you feel comfortable and where there are plenty of people around.

Fourthly, let a friend or family member know about your plans. Share your date's profile, the time, and the location of your meeting. It's always better to have someone know your whereabouts, just in case something goes wrong.

Another critical safety tip is to listen to your gut. If something feels off about a person or situation, it probably is. Don't ignore any red flags and never compromise your comfort or safety for the sake of being polite.

Moreover, it's essential to maintain a balanced perspective while dating. Don't rush into a relationship just because you feel lonely or pressured. Take your time to get to know the person, their values, and their intentions. Remember, a healthy relationship is built on mutual respect and understanding, not desperation or haste.

Lastly, don't forget to protect your emotional well-being. Online dating can be a rollercoaster of emotions. It's easy to get carried away with the thrill of meeting someone new, but it's important to stay grounded. Don't let rejection or disappointment affect your self-esteem. Remember, not every match is meant to turn into a relationship, and that's okay.

In conclusion, Facebook dating can be a fun and rewarding experience if navigated with caution and wisdom. Prioritize your safety, trust your instincts, and don't rush the process.

After all, your well-being is paramount, and any potential match should respect and understand that. These tips are not meant to scare you away from online dating, but rather to equip you with the knowledge to date safely and successfully.

So, as you venture into the world of Facebook dating, keep these tips in mind. Happy dating!

Chapter 14: Dating After a Breakup

Healing After a Breakup

In the wake of a relationship's end, it's natural to feel a whirlwind of conflicting emotions. You may feel heartbroken, confused, and lonely. It may seem like your world has crumbled, and you're left in the ruins, unsure of how to pick up the pieces. But believe me, healing after a breakup is not only possible but essential, and you are not alone in this journey.

While it might seem tempting to wallow in your sorrow, it's crucial to remind yourself that the end of a relationship is not the end of the world. It's a new beginning, an opportunity to rediscover yourself and build a stronger, more resilient version of you. The first step towards healing is to accept your feelings. It's okay to grieve. It's okay to feel hurt. These feelings are a testament to the love you had, and they validate your pain.

Once you've acknowledged your feelings, it's time to let them out. Don't bottle up your emotions; instead, express them. Talk to a friend, write in a journal, or seek professional help if necessary. By articulating your feelings, you're not only venting your frustrations but also understanding them better, which is a significant step towards healing.

While it's important to confront your feelings, it's equally crucial not to dwell on them. Don't let the breakup define you. You are so much more than a relationship that didn't work out. Focus on the positive aspects of your life, the people who love you, your passions, and your dreams.

An effective way to shift your focus from the past to the present is to engage in activities you love. Whether it's painting, hiking, reading, or cooking, immerse yourself in what brings you joy and satisfaction. This not only distracts you from the pain but also boosts your self-esteem and reminds you of your worth.

Another critical part of the healing process is self-care. It's not just about spa days and bubble baths, although those are great. It's about taking care of your physical, mental, and emotional health. Eat well, exercise regularly, get enough sleep, and take time to relax and recharge. When you take care of yourself, you send a powerful message to your brain: "I matter. I am worth it."

Lastly, forgiveness is a powerful tool in healing after a breakup. Forgive your ex for the pain they caused, forgive the relationship for not working out, and most importantly, forgive yourself for any mistakes you think you made. Forgiveness doesn't mean forgetting or condoning the hurt; it means freeing yourself from the burden of resentment and bitterness.

Healing after a breakup is a journey, not a destination. It takes time, patience, and a lot of self-love. But as you navigate through this challenging period, remember that each step you take is a step towards a better, stronger, and happier you. And when you're ready, the world of Facebook Dating awaits, teeming with potential partners who could be the right fit for you. But for now, focus on healing and rebuilding, because you deserve nothing less than happiness and love.

Reentering the Dating Scene

Diving back into the world of dating can seem like a daunting task, especially in the age of social media where the rules of romance have drastically changed. But fear not, because Facebook, the world's largest social networking site, is a treasure trove of potential partners just waiting to be discovered. The key to successful reentry into the dating scene lies in understanding how to harness the power of Facebook to your advantage.

Facebook is not just about reconnecting with old school friends or staying updated with the latest news. It's also a platform that offers countless possibilities for finding love. With over 2.7 billion users worldwide, Facebook provides an enormous pool of potential dates. It's like having the world's largest singles bar right at your fingertips, where you can meet people from all walks of life without even leaving your living room.

Navigating the digital dating landscape through Facebook is not as intimidating as it seems. The first step is to polish your online persona. Your Facebook profile is your first impression, and like it or not, people will judge you based on it. Make sure your profile reflects who you really are, not who you think people want you to be. A genuine profile will attract the right kind of attention and increase your chances of finding a match.

Unlike traditional dating methods, Facebook allows you to learn a lot about someone before you even start talking. You can view their interests, hobbies, and even their favorite books or movies. This information can be a great conversation starter and help you establish a connection right from the start.

But the power of Facebook Dating doesn't stop at just finding potential dates. It also provides an excellent platform for maintaining relationships. You can use it to keep the romance alive by sharing cute posts, tagging each other in funny memes, or even sending love notes through private messages.

However, it's essential to remember that while Facebook can open doors, it's still up to you to walk through them. Just like in the real world, online dating requires effort. You need to be proactive, engaging, and most importantly, respectful. Remember, the goal is not just to find a date but to find the right date.

It's also important to exercise caution when using Facebook for dating. Always respect the privacy of others and never stalk or harass anyone. Remember, everyone has the right to say no, and it's essential to respect their decision.

In conclusion, reentering the dating scene through Facebook can be a rewarding experience if done correctly.

It provides a vast pool of potential dates, allows you to learn about them before you even start talking, and offers a platform for maintaining relationships. But remember, like any tool, it's how you use it that determines your success. So, polish your profile, be proactive, engage respectfully, and most importantly, be yourself. Happy dating!

Dating with Baggage

In our modern world, everyone carries some baggage. Whether it's past relationships, personal issues, or life experiences, we all have our own share of baggage. However, carrying these around should not deter us from seeking love or companionship. This is especially true in the realm of Facebook dating.

Facebook dating allows us to connect with people from all walks of life, offering us a chance to find someone who understands, accepts, and appreciates us, baggage and all. But how can we navigate the dating scene on Facebook with our baggage in tow?

The first step is honesty. Be open about your past but do it tactfully. There is no need to share every detail of your past relationships or personal issues on the first date, or even on your Facebook profile. However, if the conversation naturally leads to these topics, do not shy away from them. Remember, your past has shaped you into who you are today. You are not your baggage, but your experiences have contributed to your growth and understanding of life and relationships.

Secondly, embrace empathy. Understand that just like you, the person you are connecting with on Facebook may also be carrying their own baggage. Empathy allows us to accept others as they are, without judgment. It helps us see that everyone has their own struggles and that these struggles do not define them.

The beauty of Facebook dating lies in its ability to connect us with individuals we might not usually meet in our daily lives. It broadens our horizons and introduces us to a variety of people, each with their own unique stories and experiences. This diversity can be a great tool in helping us understand and accept our own baggage.

Moreover, Facebook dating also provides us with the opportunity to take things slow. Unlike traditional dating, there is no pressure to rush into a relationship. You have the chance to really get to know the person, understand their experiences and how they have shaped them. This slow and steady process allows you to deal with your baggage, helping you move towards a healthier and happier relationship.

Lastly, don't let your baggage define your dating experience. It's easy to get caught up in the fear of being judged or rejected because of our past. Remember, everyone has their own baggage. It's not about finding someone without baggage, but someone who loves you enough to help you unpack. Be confident in who you are and what you bring to the table.

In conclusion, dating with baggage on Facebook is not only possible, but it can also be a rewarding experience. It allows us to connect with others on a deeper level, understanding and accepting each other's past. It gives us the chance to grow and learn, to move past our baggage and find a love that truly understands and accepts us. So, embrace your past, engage in the present, and look forward to a future filled with love and understanding.

Avoiding the Rebound

Just when you thought you've moved on, the past comes back to haunt you. It's the notorious "rebound" phase. This is a common pitfall for many who venture into the world of Facebook dating. However, the key to success lies in your ability to navigate this stage and avoid falling back into old patterns.

The rebound phase is often a result of residual feelings and unresolved issues with an ex. It's a period where you might find yourself yearning for the familiar, the comfortable, the 'known'. It's a time when you might be tempted to revisit old conversations, rekindle old flames, or even find a replacement for your ex. But remember, rebounds are often short-lived and rarely lead to long-term satisfaction.

The beauty of Facebook dating is that it offers a fresh start. It provides an opportunity to meet new people, explore new interests, and perhaps even discover a new side of yourself. It's a chance to redefine your love life, on your terms. However, this fresh start can quickly turn into a messy rerun if you let the rebound phase take control.

So, how do you avoid the rebound when dating on Facebook?

Firstly, give yourself time to heal. It's important to remember that it's okay to be single. Use this time to reflect on your past relationship, identify what went wrong, and what you can do better in the future. This introspection will not only help you avoid repeating the same mistakes but also prepare you for a healthier relationship.

Secondly, establish clear boundaries. If you find yourself constantly checking your ex's Facebook profile or engaging in conversations with them, it's time to set some limits. Unfriend or block them if necessary. This might seem harsh, but it's crucial for your emotional wellbeing.

Thirdly, avoid jumping into a new relationship too quickly. While it might be tempting to find a quick fix for your loneliness, rushing into a new relationship can often lead to more heartbreak. Instead, focus on building a strong foundation of friendship before moving onto romance.

Lastly, use Facebook dating as a tool for personal growth. Use this platform to learn more about different people, cultures, and perspectives. Engage in meaningful conversations, participate in diverse activities, and broaden your horizons. This will not only enhance your dating experience but also help you grow as an individual.

Remember, the goal of Facebook dating is not to replace your ex but to find someone who complements you. It's about finding a partner who respects you, understands you, and loves you for who you are. So, don't let the rebound phase cloud your judgment or hinder your chances of finding true love.

In conclusion, avoiding the rebound when dating on Facebook is all about self-care, setting boundaries, and taking things slow. It's about prioritizing your emotional wellbeing and making conscious choices. With these strategies in mind, you can navigate the world of Facebook dating with confidence and poise, setting the stage for a fulfilling love life.

Finding Love Again

In the aftermath of a painful breakup, the prospect of finding love again may seem daunting. You may feel reluctant to plunge back into the dating pool, fearing the potential heartbreak or loss. However, let us assure you, love can indeed be found again, and this time, it could be even more fulfilling and enduring. This chapter will guide you on how to use Facebook Dating to find love again.

Facebook Dating, unlike other dating platforms, provides a unique medium for people to connect and find love. The platform is integrated into the main Facebook app, making it easily accessible and convenient for users. It offers a range of features designed to help you find a match based on your interests, preferences, and mutual friends, thereby increasing the chances of compatibility.

Finding love again starts with openness to new possibilities. You are not the same person you were in your last relationship. You have grown, learned, and evolved, and so your partner should reflect this new you. Facebook Dating allows you to filter your potential matches based on shared interests, making it easier to find someone who resonates with your current self.

Next, it is crucial to approach dating with a positive mindset. Remember, every person you meet is a potential partner, but they could also become a good friend or a valuable connection. Facebook Dating encourages you to view dating as an exciting journey rather than a stressful task. It allows you to interact with potential matches in a relaxed environment, which can lead to more authentic connections.

The platform also values your privacy and safety. You have complete control over who can see your dating profile, and your conversations are separate from your regular Facebook Messenger chats. This feature ensures that you can explore the dating scene without worrying about unwanted attention or intrusion.

Importantly, Facebook Dating prompts you to be honest and genuine in your interactions. It asks for your real name, encourages you to share your true interests, and discourages the use of filters and edited photos. This honesty is fundamental in finding a loving and lasting relationship.

Moreover, Facebook Dating encourages you to take things slow. You can like someone's profile and start a conversation with them without any pressure to meet immediately. This approach gives you time to get to know the person better before deciding to take things to the next level.

Finally, remember that finding love again is not a race. It is about finding someone who compliments you, understands you, and loves you for who you are. Facebook Dating provides you with the tools to find this person, but it is up to you to use them wisely.

In conclusion, Facebook Dating is a revolutionary platform that can help you find love again. It encourages you to be open, positive, genuine, and patient in your search for love. So, why not give it a try? You never know, your next love story might just be a click away.

Chapter 15: Conclusion: The Future of Facebook Dating

The Evolution of Online Dating

In the vast panorama of human interaction, the advent of the internet has indubitably revolutionized the way we connect, communicate, and court. It has transformed the landscape of love, and in the heart of this transformation is the evolution of online dating. As we delve into the compelling chronicles of digital romance, we will understand how online dating has evolved and why Facebook, with its unique features and extensive user base, holds a promising potential in this realm.

In the late 90s, with the onset of the digital age, online dating emerged as a novel concept. It was a time when the internet was still finding its footing, and people were learning to navigate this new world. The first online dating platforms were simple, allowing users to create profiles and search for potential matches. However, they were often stigmatized, seen as a last resort for those unable to find love in the traditional ways.

Yet, as the internet became more ingrained in our daily lives, so did the acceptance of online dating. The early 2000s saw the rise of dating websites like eHarmony and OkCupid, which used complex algorithms to match users based on compatibility. These platforms emphasized the seriousness of dating, aiming to connect people for long-term relationships.

However, the real game-changer came in 2012 with the launch of Tinder. This app introduced the concept of swiping, making online dating a casual, game-like experience. The emphasis shifted from lengthy profiles and compatibility tests to quick, image-based judgments. Online dating became more mainstream, appealing to younger audiences who appreciated the speed and simplicity of the swipe.

Fast forward to today, online dating is a multi-billion dollar industry, with a myriad of platforms catering to diverse preferences and lifestyles. The stigma once associated with it has largely dissipated, replaced by the recognition that online dating is merely another avenue to find love, not a sign of desperation.

Now, Facebook, the social media behemoth, has entered the online dating scene. With its launch of Facebook Dating, it poses a significant challenge to existing platforms. Its unique edge? The power of social networking. Facebook Dating leverages the extensive data it has on its users, from their likes, dislikes, interests, and social circles, to offer potential matches. Unlike other platforms, it doesn't rely solely on images or superficial swipes.

Moreover, Facebook's vast user base, spanning across all ages and demographics, provides a larger pool of potential matches. Its integration with other Facebook features like Events and Groups facilitates more natural, interest-based interactions. It also addresses safety concerns with features like the ability to share your date details with a trusted friend.

To sum up, the evolution of online dating has been a fascinating journey. From the early days of profile browsing to the swiping frenzy, it has continually adapted to the changing needs and preferences of its users. Now, with Facebook entering the fray, online dating is set for another transformation. Leveraging its vast user data and social networking capabilities, Facebook Dating has the potential to redefine the online dating experience, making it more personalized, inclusive, and safe. So, are you ready to uncover the secrets of Facebook Dating and explore this new frontier of digital love?

Potential Changes to Facebook Dating

As we delve further into the exciting world of Facebook Dating, it's crucial to anticipate potential changes that might occur in this platform. Facebook is known for its commitment to enhancing user experience, and as such, it's not far-fetched to expect some alterations in the near future. This chapter will explore some potential changes that might revolutionize your Facebook Dating experience.

One of the possible changes could be a more personalized dating experience. Currently, Facebook Dating operates on a simple algorithm that matches you with people based on your interests and preferences. However, as technology continues to evolve, we can expect Facebook to implement more advanced AI algorithms. These algorithms could analyze your online behavior, conversations, and reactions to different profiles to provide a more personalized and accurate matching process.

Another potential change could be the integration of virtual reality (VR) technology. Imagine going on virtual dates, where you can interact with your match in a virtual space. This could add a whole new level of fun and excitement to your dating experience. It's also a great way to break the ice and get to know your match before meeting them in person. While this might seem like a concept from a sci-fi movie, remember that Facebook owns Oculus, a leading VR company. So, it's entirely possible that VR dating could become a part of Facebook Dating.

In addition, the introduction of video profiles could be another exciting change. Video profiles can give you a better understanding of a person's character, interests, and lifestyle. They can also help you express your personality in a more dynamic way. In a world where online authenticity is highly valued, video profiles could be a game-changer in online dating.

Moreover, Facebook Dating could also introduce more safety features. As online dating platforms become increasingly popular, they also become targets for scams and frauds. Facebook might introduce features like profile verification, real-time photo analysis, and AI-powered scam detection. These features could make your dating experience safer and more secure.

Lastly, Facebook Dating might also enhance its compatibility tests. These tests could take into account factors like personality traits, values, life goals, and even astrological signs. The goal would be to provide you with matches that are not just interesting, but also compatible with you on a deeper level.

In conclusion, the world of Facebook Dating is likely to evolve in the coming years. These potential changes could make your dating experience more personalized, exciting, safe, and effective. However, it's important to remember that while these changes have the potential to enhance your dating experience, the key to successful online dating still lies in authenticity, honesty, and open communication. So, stay true to yourself, embrace the changes, and let Facebook Dating guide you to your perfect match.

The Role of AI in Dating

In today's digital age, the quest for love has been revolutionized by technology, opening up an entirely new world of dating possibilities. Facebook, the social networking giant, is at the forefront of this revolution, leveraging the power of artificial intelligence (AI) to redefine the dating landscape.

Imagine a world where your dating prospects are not just based on your preferences but also on your online behavior, interests, and mutual friends. This is not a distant future, but a reality made possible by AI technology embedded in Facebook Dating.

AI has the power to sift through a mountain of data to find the perfect match for you. It takes into account your likes, shares, and even the content of your posts to understand your personality better. In essence, AI becomes your personal matchmaker, analyzing your online behavior to connect you with potential partners who share similar interests, values, and lifestyle.

Facebook Dating uses AI to suggest matches not just based on age, location, and a few shared interests, but also on a multitude of factors that contribute to compatibility. The algorithm takes into account the pages you like, the posts you share, and the groups you are part of. It even considers your interaction with other users to suggest matches. This level of personalization is possible only because of the power of AI.

But the role of AI in Facebook Dating goes beyond just suggesting matches. It also helps in facilitating meaningful conversations. Once you match with someone, Facebook Dating uses AI to suggest conversation starters based on the common interests and mutual friends. This not only breaks the ice but also fosters deeper, more meaningful conversations right from the start.

AI also plays a crucial role in ensuring the safety and security of users on Facebook Dating. It uses intelligent algorithms to detect and remove fake profiles, reducing the risk of scams and ensuring a safer dating environment.

Facebook Dating also takes user privacy seriously. It uses AI to recommend matches without sharing your activity with your Facebook friends. This ensures that your dating life remains separate from your Facebook profile, providing you with the privacy you need.

Moreover, Facebook Dating uses AI to continuously learn and improve. The more you use it, the better it gets at suggesting matches that align with your preferences and lifestyle. This means that as you continue to use Facebook

Dating, your chances of finding the perfect match only increase.

In conclusion, AI has transformed the world of dating, making it more personalized, secure, and efficient. By harnessing the power of AI, Facebook Dating offers a unique and enriching dating experience that goes beyond the traditional boundaries. It's not just about finding a date; it's about finding the right one.

So, if you are tired of the traditional dating apps and are looking for a more personalized and meaningful dating experience, give Facebook Dating a try. Let the power of AI guide you in your quest for love, helping you find the perfect match who shares your interests, values, and lifestyle. After all, love is not just about finding the right person, but also about the journey of discovery. And with AI at your side, this journey becomes all the more exciting and fulfilling.

The Impact of Social Media on Relationships

In the captivating world of digital connectivity, social media has emerged as an undeniable force, transforming the way we communicate, interact, and even form relationships.

This revolution has especially been felt in the realm of dating, where platforms like Facebook have introduced a new dynamic in human connections. This chapter delves into the profound impact of social media on relationships, particularly focusing on Facebook dating.

The advent of Facebook dating has democratized the world of romance, enabling individuals to explore prospective partners beyond their immediate geographical confines. You can now connect with someone from a different city, country, or even continent, and cultivate a relationship. This global connectivity has led to an increase in intercultural relationships, fostering diversity and broadening our understanding of love and companionship.

Moreover, Facebook dating has also introduced a new level of convenience and accessibility. Gone are the days when finding love meant physically going out and meeting people. Now, you can reach out to potential partners right in the comfort of your home, or on the go. This convenience can be particularly beneficial for individuals with demanding careers or those who live in remote areas.

However, while the benefits are numerous, Facebook dating also presents its share of challenges. The virtual platform can sometimes foster superficial connections based on profile pictures and brief bios, rather than deep, meaningful relationships built on shared experiences and personal interaction. It's easy to get lost in the sea of potential matches, and the constant availability of options can lead to a lack of commitment.

The anonymity of online interactions can also embolden individuals to misrepresent themselves, creating false personas that may not reflect their true character or intentions. Catfishing, where individuals use fake profiles to deceive others, is a common concern in the world of Facebook dating. It's important, therefore, to approach online dating with a healthy dose of skepticism and caution.

Another significant aspect to consider is the impact of social media on existing relationships. Facebook, with its constant updates and notifications, can sometimes act as a third wheel in a relationship, causing distractions and fostering insecurity. The public nature of Facebook can also lead to oversharing, which can cause conflict and misunderstanding in relationships.

Despite these challenges, it's undeniable that Facebook dating has revolutionized the way we form and maintain relationships. It offers a platform to meet people you might never have crossed paths with otherwise, and it allows for a level of pre-screening that can save time and heartache.

In conclusion, while Facebook dating presents a new frontier in the world of romance, it is important to navigate it with caution. It's essential to remember that the goal is to forge genuine connections based on shared interests, values, and mutual respect. As with all things in life, balance is key: while it's okay to embrace the convenience and global reach of Facebook dating, it's equally important to invest time and effort in building meaningful, in-person relationships.

Final Thoughts

As we reach the final stages of our enlightening journey into the landscape of Facebook dating, it is important to take a moment to reflect on the insights we have gathered. The world of online dating, particularly on Facebook, is a vast and complex entity, and it is essential to navigate it with a keen sense of awareness and understanding.

The first crucial point to remember is that Facebook dating is not merely about seeking out potential partners. It is about building connections, nurturing relationships, and fostering a sense of community. It is about finding common ground with others, discovering shared interests, and creating meaningful conversations. It is about being authentic, being yourself, and showing respect for others.

However, it is equally important to remember that Facebook dating, like all forms of online dating, is not without its pitfalls. It is essential to be cautious and protect your privacy. It is also crucial to be aware of potential scams and dishonest individuals who may try to take advantage of you. Always trust your instincts and take your time to get to know someone before getting too involved.

Yet, most importantly, remember that Facebook dating is merely a tool. It is a means to an end, not the end itself. It is a platform that can help you connect with others, but it is not a replacement for genuine, face-to-face interactions. It is a stepping stone, a way to meet new people and broaden your horizons, but it is not a guarantee of love or happiness.

That being said, Facebook dating can be an incredibly rewarding experience if approached correctly. It can lead to new friendships, exciting experiences, and even love. But it all starts with you. You have to be willing to put in the effort, to be patient, and to be open to the possibilities.

In conclusion, let's revisit the core essence of our journey. Facebook dating offers an unparalleled opportunity to connect with a diverse range of individuals from all walks of life. It allows you to take control of your dating life and to pursue potential partners at your own pace. It enables you to break free from the constraints of traditional dating and to explore new avenues of connection.

However, it is not a magic bullet. It requires effort, patience, and a strong sense of self. It requires you to be authentic, to be respectful, and to be aware of the potential pitfalls. But if you approach it with the right mindset, with the right tools, and with the right expectations, Facebook dating can be a truly rewarding experience.

So, as we close this chapter, remember that the world of Facebook dating is at your fingertips. It is a world of endless possibilities, a world of potential connections, a world of potential love. But it is up to you to seize these opportunities, to navigate this world with care and confidence, and to make the most of what Facebook dating has to offer.

In the end, remember that love is not a destination, but a journey. And Facebook dating is just one of the many paths you can take on this journey. So go forth, explore, and enjoy the exciting world of Facebook dating. The secrets are now yours to discover.